D0033127

SEASHORE PLANTS

OF

NORTHERN CALIFORNIA

BY

E. YALE DAWSON

UNIVERSITY OF CALIFORNIA PRESS

BERKELEY, LOS ANGELES, LONDON

NOTE ON THE ILLUSTRATIONS

The cover illustration shows a rocky shore habitat at Point Lobos State Park, Monterey County, with *Lessoniopsis littoralis* and *Laminaria setchellii* exposed at low tide, together with various other seaweeds. I am indebted to the late Dr. H. E. Jaques for permission to reproduce a number of the line drawings from my *How to Know the Seaweeds*, published by the Wm. C. Brown Co. Several of the drawings are modifications of renditions by Michael Neushul. Figures 36 and 41 are by César Acleto. The remainder are original or redrawings by the author from various published sources. The color illustrations of specimens are the work of Don Ollis and Dallas Clites. J. B. Jensen contributed the first two figures of plate 1.

UNIVERSITY OF CALIFORNIA PRESS

BERKELEY AND LOS ANGELES, CALIFORNIA

UNIVERSITY OF CALIFORNIA PRESS, LTD.

LONDON, ENGLAND

CONTENTS

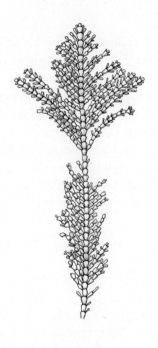

An articulated, calcareous red alga, *Corallina*.

INTRODUCTION

California is not only the most populous, but the most popular state of the nation, and its seashore is the playground, the delight, and the inspiration of millions. From Avila and Morro Bay to Moonstone Beach and the rocky islets of Trinidad, the coast of central and northern California is a world attraction of natural beauty. As the California shore has become familiar to many, its curious plants and animals of tidepool and beach have become a source of widespread interest.

Unfortunately, our marine plants have received little publicity to date, and few materials are available to the layman to help him recognize and identify the many interesting and colorful kinds that he may find. This little book is intended to portray most of the common and widespread species that occur north of Point Conception and in a way that will make them easily identified without the need of microscopic equipment or the study of wordy descriptions. You will, of course, find plants that are not pictured here, but those that are presented have been selected from long experience with the marine vegetation of this coast as the ones most frequently encountered. The explanatory notes will help with some of the less common species, and the bibliography provides sources of information of more detailed nature for those who wish to take a more advanced step into marine botany.

It must be pointed out that the collection of all plant and animal specimens on the California coast is regulated by the California Department of Fish and Game, and that it is prohibited to remove any of these things from the shore without permission. Serious students and those who wish to make collections for study should obtain a collectors' permit. Others will observe, identify and enjoy their finds, but will leave them for the next to see.

THE NORTHERN CALIFORNIA MARINE ENVIRONMENT

The California coastal waters north of Point Conception are almost uniformly cool. There are no warm currents or eddies along this part of the shore, but for the very reason of its cool character these waters richly favor the growth of marine plants, and we find some of the most magnificent stands of seaweeds in the world in this region. Much of this coast, too, is little polluted. There are abundant and varied rocky shores, tidepools and reefs, and generally an active and powerfully aerating surf. All of these factors favor the development of marine vegetation. Beds of massive kelps extend along virtually the whole coast, and intertidal vegetation is usually luxuriant wherever rocks are present for attachment. Indeed, rocky shores such as those of the Monterey Peninsula support an extraordinary diversity of seaweeds. Almost half of the seaweed species known to occur in all of California may be found at the Monterey peninsula. There are many other excellent rocky shore areas in which diversified collections may be made. A few outstanding ones are Cayucos and San Simeon in San Luis Obispo County, Moss Beach and Pigeon Point in San Mateo County, Bolinas in Marin County, and Trinidad in Humboldt County.

Seashore plants are best observed at low tide when the light is good. Such conditions do not always occur at convenient times, for on our coast the good low tides of summer come very early in the morning, mostly before or just after sunrise. The low "minus" tides of the autumn, however, occur in the afternoon, and some of the most enjoyable field excursions can be made during our fine weather of October and November. Fortunately, good seaweeding can also be done when the tide is not low, for frequently one encounters on the sand piles of drifted seaweeds cast up from the sublittoral region. Many different species, including the colorful ones of deeper water, may be found in such drift, especially after the first fall storms, and it is both interesting and convenient to pick them out on a sunny afternoon as the tide recedes. By collecting the driftweed early and then the attached plants of a reef as the tide ebbs, one may obtain the widest selection of species common both to the intertidal and to the deeper waters. To do this, one should plan to arrive at the shore two or three hours before the predicted time of a low tide.

HOW TO COLLECT AND MOUNT SEASHORE PLANTS

Collection and preservation of seaweed specimens is simple, and one may keep preserved material for long periods of time without mounting if a suitable container is used. It is easiest to collect specimens in plastic bags and to pickle them in a mixture of seawater and formaldehyde (about 19 parts seawater to 1 part commercial formaldehyde). If the specimens are to be kept for some time before mounting, they should be placed in a tight metal can or, if in glass, at least in a very dark place. Bleaching from light may otherwise quickly have a bad effect.

Mounting also is easy, but requires a few special materials. Specimens are prepared by spreading and pressing them onto a piece of high-quality rag paper. Regular herbarium paper may be obtained from Commercial Paper Corp., 300 Brannan Street, San Francisco. A standard plant press and drying felts should also be at hand.

The pickled seaweeds are floated out in a little tap water in a broad, white enamel pan or in a sink, and the paper to be used as backing placed under them in the water. A very slight depth of water is sufficient to wet the paper and to spread and arrange the specimen on it. The paper is then withdrawn with its specimen, drained momentarily and laid on a drying felt in the press. It may then be covered with a sheet of household waxed paper or a piece of cotton sheeting and another drying felt placed on top for the next specimen. When the pile of materials is complete, the press is strapped up and the drying allowed to proceed. The wet felts should be replaced with dry ones at least once a day until the specimens are dry. Fresh, living material may be treated in much the same way, but drying will be faster if the plants are killed and fixed in formalin before mounting.

After the specimens are dried on their backing sheets, they may be provided with appropriate labels, indicating place, date, and conditions of collecting, and mounted further on standard herbarium sheets of uniform size. Some people prefer to keep their smaller specimens in albums, but standard herbarium filing is the better long-term procedure.

Many marine algae are delicate plants whose characters can only be determined microscopically. These may often have to be preserved in liquid and prepared on microscope slides for study. For purposes of the present book, however, attention will be confined to the larger forms which may be recognized by their gross characteristics.

WHAT ARE THE SEAWEEDS?

The larger plants of the sea are almost exclusively members of a diversified assemblage known as algae. The various groups of algae include a great many

In addition to the algae there are a few kinds of small freshwater forms and marine species ranging from microscopic, unicellular ones to the giant kelps. We are concerned here with only three principal groups which include nearly all the macroscopic seaweeds, and these are known by the predominant colors which many of their members assume. Thus, we have the Green Algae (Chlorophyta) of which most members are of a distinctly green color (pl. 1, a); the Brown Algae (Phaeophyta) of which most are of a brownish color (pl. 1; pl. 4, 9; pl. 7, 6), including the large kelps; and the Red Algae (Rhodophyta) which are often reddish, but may also have other pigments which lend a purplish, yellowish, greenish, or brownish color (pl. 2, c; pl. 6; pl. 7a).

All of the algae are spore-producing plants, and the spores are microscopic. Reproductive organs, in fact, are mostly to be seen only with a microscope, but for critical identification of species they usually must be examined. Some of the reproductive structures are sufficiently conspicuous that they will be mentioned in the following pages, and the student will often find that a simple hand lens will reveal many interesting and distinctive features invisible to the naked eye.

The algae in most cases have complex life histories that include an alternation of a sexual, gamete-producing generation with a spore-producing generation. Thus, a single species may consist of three different plants, a male gametophyte plant, a female gametophyte plant, and a sporophyte plant (fig. 1). Usually these different plants resemble one another closely, but in some cases, such as the giant kelps, the sexual plants are exceedingly minute and observable only microscopically. In a few cases the sexual and the spore-producing plants are dissimilar and look like different species. In this book, only the common, conspicuous plants are presented for easy recognition.

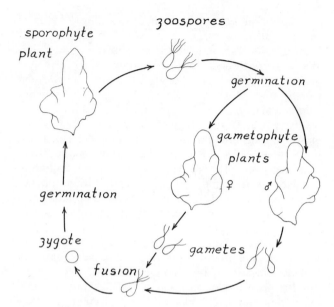

Fig. 1. Life history of *Ulva*, showing alternation of generations.

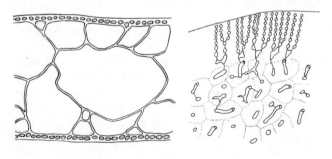

Fig. 2. Examples of cellular structure in marine algae: left, thin, definite walls of both large and small cells; right, indefinite, gelatinous walls within which the cell contents occupy small oval or elongate cavities connected by minute strands of protoplasm.

In addition to the algae there are a few kinds of flowering plants in the sea. We have three kinds in northern California, generally referred to as "eel grass." However, both true eel grass and surf grasses occur in different habitats (see p. 82-88). These curious marine grasses produce true flowers and seeds.

STRUCTURE AND REPRODUCTION OF MARINE ALGAE

The macroscopic marine algae belong to three principle divisions or phyla designated by color as indicated above: Chlorophyta: Green Algae; Phaeophyta: Brown Algae; Rhodophyta: Red Algae. The colors will prove most helpful to the user of this book as a means of finding the main assemblage to which a plant belongs.

The algae have no true roots, leaves, or flowers. Although parts of many larger algae resemble roots or leaves, we treat the entire plant body of the alga as a *thallus*. We call the attaching portions the *holdfast*, the erect, stem-like stalk, the *stipe*. The leafy parts are the *blades*. Some algae have finely dissected thalli in which neither stipe nor blade can be recognized. All have holdfasts, however, except where the plant has broken loose and becomes free-floating for a time.

Apart from a small number of green algae of multinucleate, noncellular structure, the seaweeds are composed of definite cells which often have a precise and distinctive shape and arrangement. Many of the identifying characters of the algae are to be found in the cell structure, and there are great diversities in this respect. Some simple forms consist of a single branched row of cells; some of a sheet of cells in one or two layers. Some are composed mainly of equidiametrical cells while others have tissues made up of elongate, filamentous chains of cells. The cell walls may be thin and definite, or sometimes very thick, gelatinous, and indefinite (fig. 2).

[11]

The kind of branching of the thallus may often be distinctive and readily recognized (fig. 3). The manner of development of the thallus from terminal, basal, or lateral meristems provides special distinctive features, and the character of the apex of branches, whether with a single apical cell or a multicellular growing point, must often be determined in making identifications of genera and species (fig. 4).

The algae are all cryptogams of "hidden reproduction." They are spore producers lacking the familiar reproductive structures of flowering seed plants. The spores are of two principal kinds: motile and non-motile. In the green and brown algae the spores are usually motile, flagellated unicells called *zoospores* (see fig. 1). They are produced in various ways and positions in *sporangia*. In the Red Algae the spores are all non-motile and usually are produced in groups of four *tetraspores*. These are in several distinct arrangements useful in classification (fig. 5).

As indicated above, the spores produced by the sporophyte plants usually give rise, not to more sporophyte plants, but to sexual (gametophyte) plants, often male and female. In the green and brown algae the sexual plants for the most part produce motile, flagellate gametes, often similar to the zoospores. The male and female gametes may be similar or different in size, or the female may be non-motile and fertilized by a much smaller male gamete. In the Red Algae none of the gametes is motile. The small male *spermatium* fertilizes a female gamete that does not leave the female plant, and the zygote undergoes a complex development before producing another kind of spore, called *carpospore*, which in turn reproduces the sporophyte generation (fig. 6).

The examination of cellular structure and of these finer details in the algae requires the preparation of microscope slides bearing small portions of plants or cut sections which can be examined with a compound microscope. This kind of investigation may be carried out by those who wish to go beyond the scope of this introductory book. They may undertake more extensive collection and study through the use of such comprehensive literature as is listed in the bibliography on page 82.

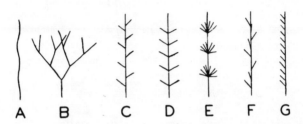

Fig. 3. Kinds of branching: A, simple (without branches); B, dichotomous; C, alternate; D, opposite; E, verticillate; F, polystichous; G, secund.

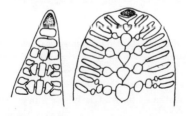

Fig. 4. Two types of growing points with apical cells.

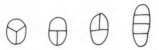

Fig. 5. Some arrangements of tetraspores in tetrasporangia: left to right, zonate, cruciate, cruciate, tetrahedral.

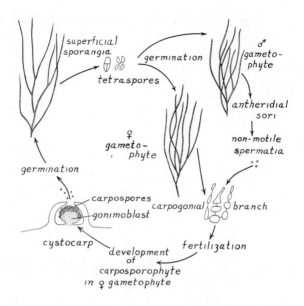

Fig. 6. Life history of the red alga, *Gracilaria*.

COLOR KEY TO THE MAJOR GROUPS OF MARINE ALGAE

1. Color distinctly green (grass green, dark green, or yellowish green) .... Green Algae (Chlorophyta)
1. Color not at all distinctly green 2
   2. Color distinctly brown (dark brown to yellowish brown,
      but not reddish .... Brown Algae (Phaeophyta)
   2. Color generally red or reddish, but variable, sometimes
      purplish or very dark, dull reddish to almost blackish,
      rarely greenish, occasionally brownish, but with a red-
      dish tinge and reddish spores..Red Algae (Rhodophyta)

THE GREEN ALGAE (CHLOROPHYTA)

The members of this phylum, which includes many freshwater forms, are easily recognized by their grass-green color. Only rarely do members of other seaweed groups show a distinctly green color. Although most Chlorophyta are grass-green, a few are very dark green and some are yellowish-green.

These algae are mostly small to moderate in size, only exceptionally exceeding a foot in greatest dimension. Some are finely branched, filamentous or tufted plants; other are broad, membranous sheets. Most are intertidal species, and a few, such as *Ulva* and *Enteromorpha*, are among the most frequently encountered algae in quiet bays, harbors, and boat landings. There are not so many kinds of green algae to be found in northern California, compared with Phaeophyta and Rhodophyta, but some of them are exceedingly abundant.

Ulva (from the Celtic) Sea Lettuce

The various species of *Ulva* are among the most conspicuous of intertidal algae by manner of their bright green color and their abundance in many situations. *Ulva* is especially common in bays, lagoons, harbors, and marshes, but at certain seasons covers much of the middle levels of many exposed shores (pl. 1, a). *U. lactuca* is perhaps the commonest of several almost cosmopolitan species (fig. 7). Together with *U. expansa* it may develop very expansively in quiet water of salt marshes and shallow bays to form large, undulate, detached sheets that at low tide are left spread on the mud.

Ulva is easy to recognize as a thin, green, membranous thallus of only two layers of cells, but the species usually are difficult to distinguish. *U. taeniata*, however, is a very distinctive one characterized by long, narrow, twisted and ruffled segments with teeth along the lower margins.

As one of the oldest generic names among the seaweeds, *Ulva* was established by Linnaeus in 1753.

Enteromorpha (intestine shape)

Enteromorpha is closely related to *Ulva* and differs mainly in being hollow. Thus, the hollow tube of *Enteromorpha* consists of a single layer of cells (fig. 8) while the membrane of *Ulva* resembles a collapsed *Enteromorpha* in which the opposing walls have become adherent to each other.

Enteromorpha is a cosmopolitan genus which may be encountered in almost any shallow-water marine environment. It is especially prevalent on boat hulls, buoys, docks, and woodwork. It is commonly associated with *Ulva* in bays and marsh waterways. It has considerable tolerance for fresh water.

One of the commonest species is *E. intestinalis* which is an unbranched one arising solitarily from

Fig. 7. *Ulva lactuca*, × 0.5.

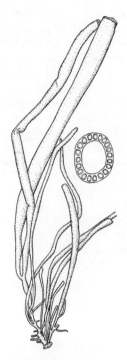

Fig. 8. *Enteromorpha* species with basal branching, × 1;
hollow structure of a small branch, × 10.

a small holdfast. It shows a contorted and irregularly
swollen character suggesting a piece of intestine.

Other common species, such as *E. compressa*, are
branched, mainly at the base (fig. 8). Species recognition among these branched plants is very difficult
because of exceeding variability and the fact that the
really distinctive characters must be sought in the
life histories rather than in external form. Some cannot be distinguished without study of the living, motile gametes and zoospores.

[17]

Cladophora (branch bearing)

This is a large genus of numerous species both in the marine and the freshwater environments. It is fairly readily recognized by its uniseriate, branched filaments in which the septa occur at rather close intervals and at the base of every branch. It lacks hooked branchlets. Most of the plants are quite delicate forms seldom reaching more than a few inches in length. They have mostly been distinguished on cell size, cell shape, and branching, but some are so variable that they present considerable difficulties in

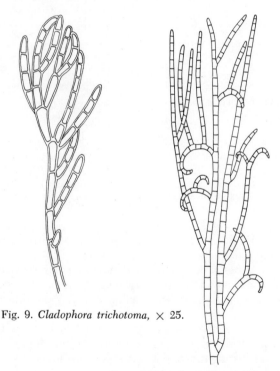

Fig. 9. *Cladophora trichotoma,* × 25.

Fig. 10. *Spongomorpha coalita,* × 7.

classification. One of the common and distinctive ones in California is *C. trichotoma* (fig. 9) which grows at fairly high intertidal levels as a densely congested, spongy, hemispherical tuft an inch or so high and capable of holding sufficient water (together with sand) in the intricate network of its abundant branches so that it can readily withstand lengthy periods of tidal exposure without drying out.

Spongomorpha (sponge shape)

This finely and abundantly branched filamentous plant has the appearance of a piece of much-frayed green rope. It reaches a foot or more in length and may be encountered in a variety of intertidal and shallow-water environments. The entangled, congested character of the branches results from the holding ability of multitudes of short, prong-like, recurved branchlets (fig. 10). The plant is otherwise much like a species of *Cladophora* in consisting of branched, regularly septate filaments.

Bryopsis (moss-like)

This genus is one of the few in our area in which the thallus is not divided up into discrete cells. The branched axes, instead, consist of a tough, flexible cell wall forming a hollow, ramified tube filled with protoplasm that flows from one part of the plant to another.

Bryopsis corticulans is probably the commonest of several species that may be encountered along northern California. It forms dense, dark, soft clumps 2-3 inches high of numerous, delicate, pinnately-branched axes (fig. 11). It usually grows in surfy places and is our only green alga of such branching habit.

Codium (Greek, skin of an animal) Sponge Weed

This is another of the non-cellular coenocytes, but has a completely different structure from *Bryopsis*. *Codium fragile* is the most abundant species and is our most massive green alga, reaching a length of a foot or more and a weight of several pounds (fig. 12). Its texture is spongy and results from an interwoven mass of fine filaments which end at the surface in closely-packed, small, bladder-like swellings, each with a sharp point. It is deep green in color, cylindrical in form, and dichotomously branched. It occurs as an individual, drooping plant here and there on lower level intertidal rocks and will not be mistaken for any other alga.

There are many different kinds of *Codium* throughout warm and temperate parts of the world. Some are hollow sponges, and some are mat-like forms on rock surfaces. (We have one of these latter in northern California, *C. setchellii*.) One of the branched codiums in Baja California becomes rope-like and up to 25 feet long.

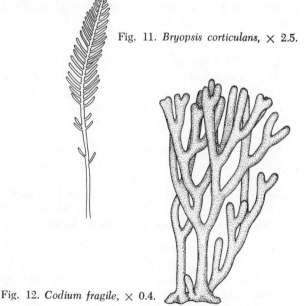

Fig. 11. *Bryopsis corticulans*, × 2.5.

Fig. 12. *Codium fragile*, × 0.4.

THE BROWN ALGAE (PHAEOPHYTA)

California is one of the few outstanding brown-algal regions of the world. Our famous beds of Giant Bladder Kelp and Bull Kelp, recently of great commercial importance, extend along almost all parts of our coast and harbor a great diversity of animal life and other associated plants.

Brown algae are best developed in temperate and cold waters. Northern California has a particularly large number of genera and species. Some twenty genera occur commonly north of Point Conception, and the principal species of each of these will be taken up below. Nearly all of them are plants of fairly large size, and some are among the largest of all the algae. Most have a distinctive habit, branching, or shape, so recognition is relatively easy.

KEY TO THE COMMON GENERA OF BROWN ALGAE OF NORTHERN CALIFORNIA

1. Plants composed of finely branched filaments of microcopic dimensions .... *Ectocarpus*

1. Plants larger and of more firm structure, not composed of free filaments of microscopic dimensions 2

   2. Plants more or less hollow throughout.............. 3

   2. Plants not hollow throughout, although sometimes with hollow parts (air bladders).................. 4

3. Plants bubble-shaped, simple, or convoluted....*Colpomenia*

3. Plants hollow-tubular, straight, or contorted....*Scytosiphon*

   4. Plants prostrate, crust-like .... *Ralfsia*

   4. Plants erect or drooping, not crust-like 5

5. Mature plants with 1 or more hollow air bladders or vesicles 6

5. Mature plants without bladders or vesicles 9

   6. A single large bulb terminating a long, slender stipe and bearing blades from short branchlets .... *Nereocystis*

   6. Plants with many small air bladders 7

[21]

7. Plants very large, with a single air bladder at the base of many lateral blades 8

7. Plants not so large, with very small air vesicles in bead-like series .... *Cystoseira*

8. Main axes cylindrical .... *Macrocystis*

8. Main axes flat .... *Egregia*

9. Plants rather small, paper thin, unbranched and with scarcely evident stipe 10

9. Plants rather coarse and thick or large and membranous, usually branched, but if unbranched, then with a prominent stipe 11

10. Plants dark brown, strap-shaped, on rocks .... *Petalonia*

10. Plants pale brown, like a collapsed and flattened sack, epiphytic on *Cystoseira*.............*Coilodesme*

11. Plants with one or more ribs, veins, stipes, or grooves running through the principal blades 12

11. Plants without evident midrib or veins 18

12. Blades (at least the main or primary one) with a single midrib, vein, or stipe 13

12. Blades with several parallel ribs or grooves 17

13. Margin of blades with teeth or small bladelets........
.... *Desmarestia*

13. Margins of blades smooth or essentially so 14

14. Thalli dichotomously branched 15

14. Thalli not dichotomously branched, the stipe un-branched 16

15. Basal stipe parts dichotomously branched from a large, conical holdfast; blades linear .... *Lessoniopsis*

15. Entire thallus dichotomously branched .... *Fucus*

16. Stipe very stout, erect, with several large, similar blades from the upper end, the terminal one only with a broad middle stripe .... *Pterygophora*

16. Stipe not especially stout nor erect, with a group of short blades without ribs at the base of a large, long main blade with a prominent midrib .... *Alaria*

17. Plants consisting of a single stipitate blade with five prominent ribs .... *Costaria*

17. Plants consisting of a thick, cylindrical stipe with a hank of drooping terminal blades, each with numerous parallel grooves .... *Postelsia*

[22]

Ectocarpus (external fruit)

This is a large genus of small plants. Many species
of *Ectocarpus* occur as epiphytes on older, often de-
teriorating parts of a variety of other algae and even
on animals. One curious form lives on a parasitic iso-
pod attached to the tail of surf perch. Most are small,
tufted forms less than half an inch tall, but one of
the commonest species, *E. granulosus,* reaches several
inches in height and grows abundantly on intertidal
algae as a fine, brownish fleece. The thallus is composed of branched, uniseriate filaments which are
usually terminally attenuated. The tiny dark reproductive bodies can be made out with a hand lens,
but the details of these, by which many species are
distinguished, must be observed under high magnification (fig. 13).

Ralfsia (after British phycologist Ralfs)

In the middle and upper intertidal zone, on rocks
severely and frequently exposed to sun and air, is
one of the seaweeds most tolerant of desiccation.
Ralfsia lives as a dark brown or blackish crust, often
resembling a tar spot. These crusts are so firmly adherent and inflexible that they cannot be removed
intact from the rock, but can partly be scraped or cut
off with a sharp blade. The crusts begin as more or
less circular shapes, but by convergence and irregular
growth may form broad expanses a foot or more
across.

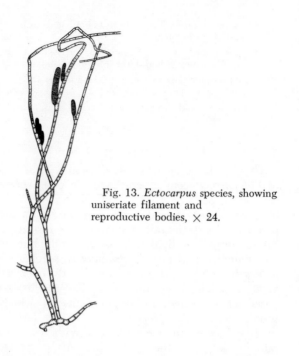

Fig. 13. *Ectocarpus* species, showing
uniseriate filament and
reproductive bodies, × 24.

The tissues of *Ralfsia* are dense and the cells are
extremely hygroscopic. The plants may become almost
crisp dry in the sun, yet remain alive and continue
growth with the first splash of the incoming tide.

There are a number of species of *Ralfsia,* but they
are poorly known and the life histories for the most
part are not recorded in the scientific literature. They
seem to produce their fruiting bodies and motile
spores and gametes mainly in winter when most in-
vestigators find it inconvenient to study algal reproduction.

Ralfsia is composed of short, erect filaments which,
however, are so densely packed and grown together
that they form a firm, solid tissue (fig. 14).

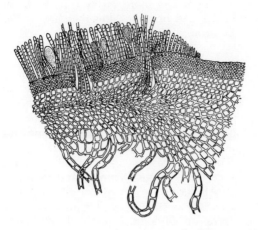

Fig. 14. *Ralfsia* species as seen in vertical section, × 58.

Desmarestia (after French naturalist Desmarest)
Acid Kelp

The seaweed collector who mixes *Desmarestia* plants with his other specimens will remember it well for the damage that ensues, for the extraordinarily high acid content of various kinds of *Desmarestia* cause marked discoloration of the pigments of other algae. It will even discolor and damage itself if a crushed or broken part is allowed to spread its acid cell sap on living surfaces.

Desmarestias are generally plants of lowermost tide levels, but they also occur down to depths of 30 feet or more. The largest specimens (to 12 feet or more) may be encountered in drift. The thalli are strap-shaped and usually characterized by a slender mid-vein with opposite branch veins. We have the large, coarse species, *D. munda,* in which the blade margins are beset with tooth-like or spine-like structures (fig.

[25]

15). *D. herbacea* is a more bushy type with shorter, smaller blades and branches, but they are all flat and tend to be arranged in a single plane.

Scytosiphon (leather tube)

This is a brown alga parallel in form with the green *Enteromorpha intestinalis* and of similar size. Our S. *lomentaria* forms tubular thalli 2-12 inches long, usually gregarious in clusters from a common, crust-like attachment. Small plants are slender and straight. Large ones tend to be inflated and irregularly constricted (pl. 4). This is a very widespread plant originally described from Denmark and found on our coast from Alaska to Mexico. It is quite strictly inter-tidal and usually occurs in our territory as the small, slender form on high-level rocks. Less frequently, larger, constricted plants are found all the way down to levels exposed only by spring tides.

Petalonia (after French biologist Petalon)

Petalonia debilis is a widely distributed alga of the high intertidal zone, originally described from Atlantic Europe, and known throughout much of the Northern Hemisphere. We find it mostly at levels of 2 to 4 feet above mean low tide mark on rocks often subject to severe desiccation. It is a dark-brown, thin, strap-like plant 6 to 12 inches long. Several blades arise from a very small holdfast disc (fig. 16). They are smooth and entire, although sometimes marginally undulate. The species is annual, appearing in the autumn and disappearing the following summer.

Colpomenia (sinuous membrane)

One of the most striking intertidal brown algae is a small, yellow-brown, hollow, bubble-like species known as *Colpomenia sinuosa* (pl. 1). This plant is widely distributed in warmer regions of the world and occurs in a variety of forms. We find it growing

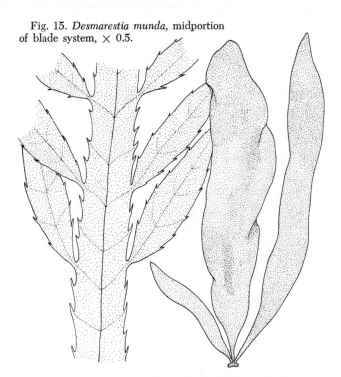

Fig. 15. *Desmarestia munda,* midportion of blade system, × 0.5.

Fig. 16. *Petalonia debilis,* habit, × 0.5.

as colonies on rocks in open places in the middle littoral, or as an epiphyte on degenerating pieces of *Egregia* or other algae. It is usually only an inch or two in diameter and of smooth, hemispherical form. However, in summer and in warm, protected areas it may become much larger, convoluted, and warty. The wall of the hollow structure is quite crisp and is usually attached very broadly to the substrate. The form and color are so distinctive that *Colpomenia* will not be confused with any other California marine plant.

[27]

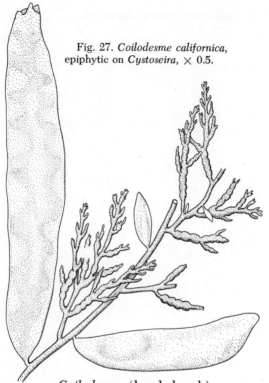

Fig. 27. *Coilodesme californica,*
epiphytic on *Cystoseira,* × 0.5.

Coilodesme (bonded sack)

This genus has a peculiar structure suggested by
its name. The plants have the form of a sack so flattened as to seem a single blade, yet, in young stages
and in some eroded conditions they are evidently
hollow. More remarkable is the fact that various species of *Coilodesme* are epiphytic only on particular
host plants. *C. californica* (fig. 17), our commonest
species, is an obligate epiphyte on *Cystoseira osmundacea* and occurs wherever the host grows. It is a
short-lived annual which appears in May and is gone
by the end of August. The thallus is usually about a
foot long and 2 to 4 inches broad.

Laminaria (a thin plate) Oar Weed

This is a genus of considerable historical and economic significance among the algea. The oar weeds were some of the most important seaweeds long ago harvested for burning down into soda ash which was used for making soap and glass. The burned ashes of these seaweeds were originally called "kelp" and we have in more recent times applied the word to various large brown algae.

Laminaria is readily recognized for it has a single unbranched stipe bearing a single blade which may be torn or split, but is not branched or provided with veins or ribs (pl. 7). The plants are quite large, some reaching a few yards in length. We have two very common species in northern California and several of lesser abundance. *L. sinclairii* is a smaller species consisting of a branched rhizome from which dense clumps of bladed stipes about a foot high arise. *L. setchellii* is a larger species, up to 4 feet tall, its stiff stipe standing erect in surfy places and supporting the hanging blade. It grows in peculiar "forests" in the surf at lowest tide levels and just below (pl. 2), and is of striking appearance on an afternoon low tide when the sun shines through the rich, brown blades and reflects from the darker stipes with each slacking of the water after a wave.

Laminaria has long been harvested for its iodine after "kelp" production became uneconomical, and in more recent decades it has become an important algin plant of Atlantic waters. Several species are common food seaweeds in the Orient (*kombu*). They are important fertilizer sources in many areas and are widely used along European coasts as stock feed.

Costaria (having longitudinal ribs)

Costaria costata (fig. 18) is a striking brown alga much like *Laminaria* in form, but provided with five prominent longitudinal ribs in the blade, two raised

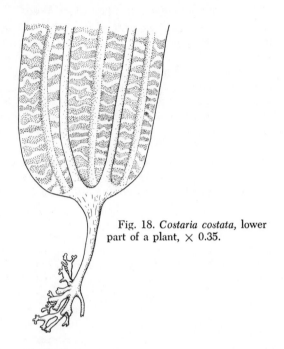

Fig. 18. *Costaria costata,* lower part of a plant, × 0.35.

on one side and three on the other. Between the ribs the blade is strongly wrinkled. It is another brown alga of the lowermost tide levels on surfy shores from Point Conception to Alaska.

Nereocystis (sea-nymph bladder) Bull Kelp

Nereocystis leutkeana is the most massive kelp of northern California. It grows up from deep water as an enormously long, rope-like stipe (to 115 feet) gradually enlarged at the top to a huge, elongate, hollow air chamber nearly six inches in diameter (fig. 19). This massive pneumatocyst supports 32–64 blades that may be 10–12 feet long and hang down in the water. Submarine groves of these giant algae show on the surface as a great many floating bulbs about the size of a sea otter's head. Indeed, it is often among the bull kelps that our sea otter herds live and feed, and one must look sharply to distinguish the two from a distance.

After a storm many bull kelps may be found littering the beaches, torn loose from their small holdfasts. Despite their size, these huge plants usually complete their growth, mature, produce spores and are cast up, all within a single year.

Macrocystis (large bladder) Giant Bladder Kelp

The Pacific coast kelp beds are famous the world over. Not only are they the most extensive and elaborate submarine forests of the world, but they have

Fig. 19. *Nereocystis leutkeana*, pneumatocyst, × 0.2.

provided for the greatest industrial seaweed production. So important is the harvest of kelp in California that it is regulated by the State Department of Fish and Game. Hundreds of thousands of dollars have been spent on kelp-bed maintenance and improvement. The principal product, algin, is utilized in so many industries that almost all of us use it in some way every day.

Macrocystis is widespread in cool waters, occurring in New Zealand, Argentina, Chile, Peru and Pacific North America, but best developed as the species *M. pyrifera* along California and northwestern Baja California. It is well known for its bladder-based, brown, wrinkled blades commonly found along the shore (fig. 20B), and for its massive tangles of stipes, blades, and holdfasts that are cast onto the beaches after a storm. The plants grow mainly in depths of 30 to 60 feet and form veritable forests in which the erect, entwined bundles of stipes resemble a tree trunk, and the spreading canopy of floating "stems and leaves" the crown of the tree (fig. 20A). *Macrocystis* anchors in sand or rocks by a huge mound of root-like haptera, and new blade-bearing stipes grow up to the surface at extraordinarily rapid rates—up to 18 inches a day. Growth in length is the fastest in the plant kingdom and exceeds that of fast-growing tropical bamboos.

The massive kelp plants are all sporophytes. They produce motile zoospores from sori on special blades in lower parts of the plant. These zoospores develop into microscopic, sexual plants which rarely grow large enough to be seen with the naked eye. These delicate male and female plantlets produce sperm and eggs which, upon fertilization, recreate the large plants of the sporophyte generation. Circumstances suitable for the growth of these minute sexual plants are critical to the survival of kelp beds.

The California kelp beds were first exploited commercially during World War I as a fertilizer resource

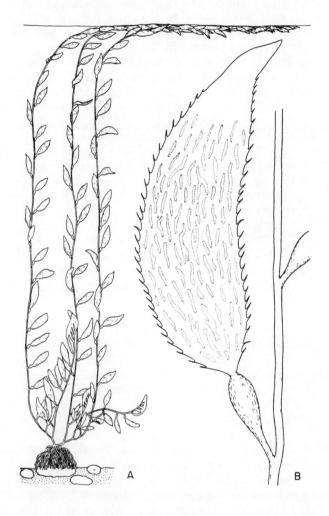

Fig. 20. *Macrocystis pyrifera*: A, habit, × 0.02; B, a blade with a basal air bladder, × 0.5.

in the absence of German potash. Various chemicals were also obtained by destructive distillation, and in the early 1930's the algin-extraction industry was developed. This has become by far the most important use of *Macrocystis* in this country. Algin is a hydrophilic colloidal substance very effective as an emulsifying and suspending agent. As such it is extensively used in the ice-cream and chocolate-milk industries and in preparing a great many processed foods. It is widely employed in paints, cosmetics, pharmaceuticals, sizings, and numerous other products.

Kelp harvesting is carried out mechanically by means of a ship designed with a mowing and hauling device by which the kelp is cut several feet below the surface and drawn up into the vessel for transport to the processing factory.

Lessoniopsis (after French naturalist Lesson)

One of the most abundant kelps of surf-swept rocky shores of California is *Lessoniopsis littoralis* which is adapted to withstand the most violent agitation of the sea. It consists of a coarse, conical, woody base attached by strong and compact haptera. The stipe is repeatedly dichotomomous and each branch terminates in a long, narrow, flat blade with a strengthening midrib (fig. 21). The whole hank of blades lashes back and forth with each wave. Unlike *Postelsia*, which lives in the same inhospitable environment, *Lessoniopsis* is perennial and may live for a number of years to become quite gnarled.

Postelsia (after Russian naturalist Postels) Sea Palm

Were we to elect a California State seaweed, this would be a fit candidate, for it is perhaps the most distinctive and striking of our intertidal algae. It has the remarkable form of a palm tree, to about 2 feet tall, with tough, thick, rubbery stipe resilient to the

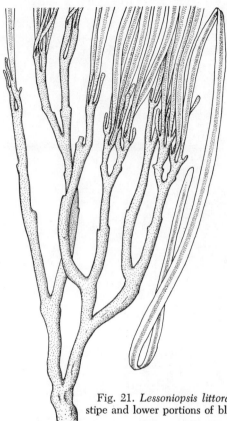

Fig. 21. *Lessoniopsis littoralis*, branched stipe and lower portions of blades, × 0.66.

most terrible pounding of the surf, and a terminal cluster of slender, drooping blades that withstand the waves like a coconut palm survives a hurricane. *Postelsia* is an annual, and in February the groves of juvenile, yellow-brown sea palms may be seen springing up reoccupy their territories among the perennial *Lessoniopsis*. The plants mature in spring and summer (fig. 22).

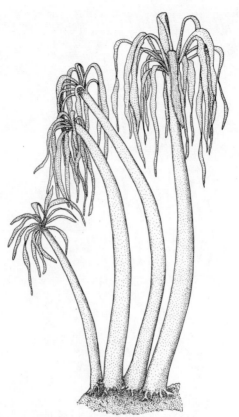

Fig. 22. *Postelsia palmaeformis*, habit, × 0.25.

One usually needs a very low tide and a calm sea in order to approach *Postelsia*, for it frequents places hardly accessible to man. Point Lobos State Park is a good place to observe it close at hand.

Pterygophora (wing-bearing)

This is another of the large, long-stiped kelps which occur mainly in deep water (20–65 feet) and may be found more commonly cast ashore in drift than intact

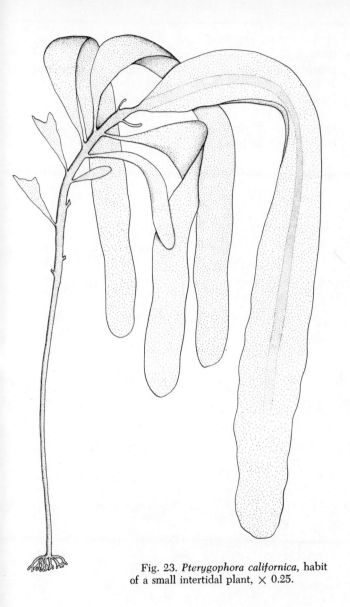

Fig. 23. *Pterygophora californica*, habit of a small intertidal plant, × 0.25.

in the lower intertidal zone. *P. californica*, the only species, has stipes about four feet long, stiff, erect, and bearing several large blades in pinnate arrangement at the top of the stipe. The main central blade has a broad, thickened stripe down its middle (fig. 23).

Pterygophora may live a number of years and develops growth rings in the stipe somewhat like the annual rings in terrestrial trees.

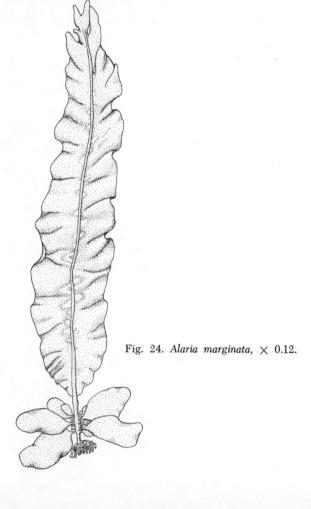

Fig. 24. *Alaria marginata*, × 0.12.

Alaria (wing)

This is a large genus of kelps of the far north Pacific region. They are best developed in large submarine beds in Alaskan and Siberian waters. Our common species, *A. marginata* (fig. 24), is one of the most southerly ones. It is often abundant at lowest intertidal levels and is easily recognized by its short stipe (1–3 inches), large, ruffled primary blade with prominent midrib, and by the several, much smaller and shorter blades (sporophylls) arising below the main blade.

Egregia (remarkably great) Feather Boa Kelp

This is another of our large kelps which can be recognized at a glance by its unique character of having long, flat, narrow axes bearing short blades and float bladders along their entire length. It is a plant of shallow, surfy waters. The axes may reach a length of 25 feet. It is a popular oddity on the beaches, and is an amusement for children who play with the strange, long feathery ropes. *Egregia menziesii* is our common and widespread species of northern California, although at Pebble Beach near Monterey a form of the southern California species, *E. laevigata* (fig. 25), also occurs. The former has rough, papillate axes, and the latter smooth ones, but they are otherwise of similar appearance.

Cystoseira (bladder chain)

Cystoseira osmundacea is a large, bushy, finely-branched brown alga 4–20 feet long that grows at mean low tide level and below. The plants have dark brown, leafy basal parts with fern-like, veined "leaves." The specific name relates to a similarity to osmunda ferns. The upper parts are much-branched, slender, and with long, stringy cylindrical axes. From spring to fall these are provided with the distinctive bead-like

Fig. 25. *Egregia laevigata,* × 0.04.

series of 5–12 small, spherical vesicles by which it is readily recognized (see fig. 17). It is commonly epiphytized by various algae, but especially by *Coilodesme californica.*

Pelvetia (after French botanist Pelvet)

The high, exposed tops of rocks in the intertidal zone are commonly draped with an olive-greenish-brown plant about a foot long (pl. 2). This is *Pelvetia fastigiata* which is adapted to a life of alternate submersion in sea water and long exposure to the air. It cannot live continually immersed, but can withstand severe desiccation. The thick, narrow branches are dichotomous, and mature, fertile plants have swollen branch tips from which the reproductive bodies are extruded from numerous pores. A closely related plant, *Hesperophycus harveyanus,* occupies about the same intertidal levels as *Pelvetia* (in our area from Point Conception to as far north as Santa Cruz) and is distinguished by a fairly distinct midrib bordered on either side by a row of white hair spots.

Pelvetiopsis (diminutive of *Pelvetia*)

At even higher levels than *Pelvetia* and *Hesperophycus,* indeed, on rocks scarcely submerged even at high tide, is a densely clustered small, light-tan-colored alga 2–3 inches tall, *Pelvetiopsis limitata.* It consists of closely dichotomous branches that tend, especially in younger stages, to be arched inwardly. Mature plants show the inflated, fertile branch tips illustrated in figure 26. *Pelvetiopsis* spends more of its life in the air than in the water, and may be collected at almost any state of the tide but the highest (pl. 2).

Fucus (ancient Greek for seaweed) Rock Weed

Until the end of the eighteenth century this ancient name was applied as a kind of generic designation to nearly all of the larger marine algae.

We have in northern California a common and exceedingly variable species, *Fucus distichus* (often

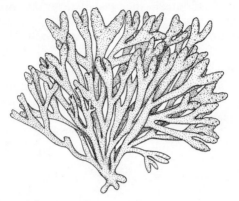

Fig. 26. *Pelvetiopsis limitata,* habit, × 0.75.

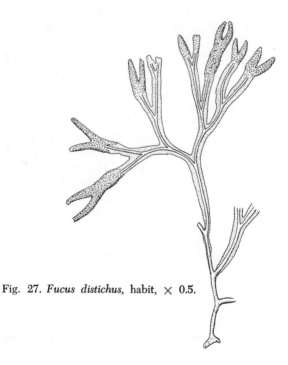

Fig. 27. *Fucus distichus,* habit, × 0.5.

called *F. furcatus*), which is widespread in the Northern Hemisphere. Like *Pelvetia*, it is a plant usually of middle and upper intertidal levels, but is distinguished by its dark brown, dichotomous blades with prominent midrib (fig. 27).

Fucus becomes more and more abundant as one goes from Point Conception (its southern limit) northward. In many northern California areas it is the dominant alga on well-exposed and somewhat elevated intertidal rocks.

THE RED ALGAE (RHODOPHYTA)

The red algae are the most abundant seaweeds of the world. There are more than 4000 species, and they occur in almost every conceivable habitat in the sea, from highest intertidal levels to the lowermost limits of light, but very few live in fresh or brackish water. Almost all grow attached to rocks or to other algae. None live in the floating state.

The Red Algae do not grow as large as some of the brown kelps, but a few reach lengths of 8–10 feet. Some of the species, especially epiphytic ones, are quite small, but almost always they are visible to the naked eye. In tropical seas the Rhodophyta tend to be mostly small forms, but in temperate waters, such as ours, the average size is from 3 to 12 inches.

One of the most interesting features of the Red Algae is their color. Although they contain green chlorophyll, that pigment is generally masked by other pigments, especially the red phycoerythrin. In brightly lighted intertidal habitats the pigments are often so dense and so mixed that a dark purplish, olive, brownish or blackish color is observed, and the beginner in phycology often confuses some of the dark-pigmented red algae with brown algae. In well-shaded places or in deeper waters, the red pigments are dominant, and the plants are almost invariably pink or red. This red color represents a specific adaptation of the plants to growth in the dim and limited light of deep water, for water absorbs red, orange, and yellow light very quickly and allows only the green and blue to penetrate to depth. The red pigment is able to absorb and use these deeply penetrating rays which are not available to other colors of algae, and they permit some Rhodophyta to live at depths as great as 600 feet.

A great majority of red seaweeds have a complex life history that includes not one, but three different plants. Thus, unlike the Brown Algae, in which the one conspicuous plant in the life history is usually the sporophyte, the red algae have, in addition to the sporophyte, a male and a female plant, and all of these are similar in size and appearance (fig. 6). This circumstance provides for many complexities in classification, for a critical identification of a given species may require the presence of the male, the female, and the spore-producing phases. In some species one can recognize the different phases easily, but in most cases microscopic examination is necessary. Female plants are most readily distinguished, for the masses of carpospores produced after sexual fertilization are visible as dark spots, lumps, or papillae in or on the thallus and are generally referred to as *crystocarps* (see fig. 44).

Sporophyte plants are most commonly encountered in a majority of species. They usually bear tetraspores. These are often produced on specialized branches or bladelets or in visible patches (sori) on the thallus.

Male plants are usually the least frequent, and their minute spermatia can be seen only under high magnification.

In the following treatment, reproductive characters will be used only where they are readily observed with no more equipment than a hand lens. Although in a local flora such as this the larger and commoner plants can be identified with relative ease, one should realize that, since many less common forms are not treated, and since exceeding variability occurs among many common ones, he cannot expect every specimen to fit either a key step or an illustration. When difficulties are encountered, one should turn to one of the more comprehensive treatises listed in the bibliography.

Key to the Common Genera of Red Algae of Northern California

43. Ultimate branchlets clustered on alternate, distichous,
    penultimate branches .... *Odonthalia*
44. Plants epiphytic on *Cystoseira;* branching alternate
    .... *Pterochondria*
44. Plants mainly in drift; branching opposite, but the
    opposite pairs dissimilar .... *Ptilota*

Smithora (after American phycologist G. M. Smith)

Although our abundant intertidal surf grass is usually emerald green, from time to time it takes on a mottled purplish color, and close examination reveals that it is covered with a small epiphytic alga. *Smithora naiadum* (fig. 28) is an obligate epiphyte on *Phyllospadix* on whose leaves it forms abundant tiny purplish, membranous blades that arise from small fleshy cushions. It was formerly thought to represent a small species of *Porphyra*, but as the life history was worked out, it proved to have a distinctive and complex reproductive cycle. It is seasonal and periodic. Sometimes only the tiny reddish cushions will be observed dotting the leaves which commonly also bear the minute crusts of *Melobesia*.

Porphyra (purple) Laver; Nori

Porphyra perforata is a red alga of extremely hygroscopic character. It is a membranous, ruffled blade without stipe, of deep, purplish color (pl. 7), and occurs usually on rocks at high levels in the *Ralfsia* and *Pelvetia* zone. *P. lanceolata* is another, larger,

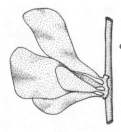

Fig. 28. *Smithora naiadum* on a leaf of *Phyllospadix*, × 5.

rock-inhabiting species, and *P. nereocystis* lives epiphytically on old *Nereocystis* pneumatocysts. These are all seasonal and best developed from late winter through summer. *Porphyra* has a gelatinous, somewhat rubbery texture when partially dehydrated, and is frequently collected by oriental Americans as a foodstuff known as nori. The Japanese nori, indeed, is the most extensively cultivated seaweed of the world and provides for an enormous marine agricultural industry involving more than 400,000 workers.

Porphyra is grown in Japan under a unique cultural procedure. The nori grounds are broad, shallow, muddy bays. At low tide during autumn, millions of bamboo poles are driven into the mud and miles of coarse-mesh nets strung on them in such a way that they are exposed at low tide. *Porphyra* spores germinate on the netting and grow into harvestable plants in a few months. Harvesting is done by hand from a narrow one-man boat that moves up and down the net lines. The nori is pulled off, dumped into a basket, collected by a mother boat and returned to the processing yards where it is chopped into fragments and spread on small mats to dry. The dry nori is removed as a thin sheet, folded or cut and packaged for market. It is consumed in large quantities as an additive in a multitude of oriental dishes. In recent times, up to 2½ billion dried sheets have been produced in a single year.

Gelidium (from *gelu,* frost; gelatin) Agarweed

The novice will find *Gelidium* one of the puzzling genera in the range of size among several of its common members. Distinctive characters, however, in the tough, cartilaginous texture and the slender, compressed form of the branches may be learned quickly, and there are some microscopic characters which make the genus easy to identify (single apical cell; minute, wire-like filaments in the medulla).

[49]

Our most abundant intertidal species is the small, tufted one, *G. coulteri*. It is a densely branched little plant 1–3 inches tall and of distichous-pinnate branching, the ultimate pinnae tending to be prong-like. It grows well exposed at middle levels, but lower down, in pools and tideways, the larger species *G. purpurascens* and *G. cartilagineum* are frequent (fig. 29). These are often characterized by young branches that resemble an arm bent at the elbow.

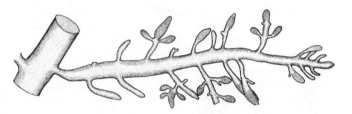

Fig. 29. *Gelidium purpurascens,* a small part of an axis with a lateral branch, × 8.

The larger species of *Gelidium* have long been the best sources of industrial agar. California plants were harvested by divers for a time during World War II when Japanese supplies were cut off. Japan is again the major refiner and exporter of finished agar which is used in many foods and pharmaceuticals, and particularly in the making of culture media for microbiological laboratories.

Hildenbrandia (after Austrian botanist Hildenbrand)

Smooth stones and eroded shells from the bottom of tide pools often exhibit what appear to be deep red stains or paint spots on the surface. These red blotches are the thin, adherent films of the non-calcareous, crustose red alga *Hildenbrandia prototypus*. It is a cosmopolitan plant, and once one is familiar with it, he will notice it on rocks almost everywhere, from the walls of sea caves and the sides of intertidal boulders to rock and shell surfaces from considerable depths. The crusts are so thin and firm that a sharp blade is required to remove even a tiny scraping. A hand lens will reveal the minute pits in the crust (conceptacles) which contain the tetrasporangia.

Petrocelis (rock overlay)

Another of the thin, rock-covering films, which are inconspicuous until one slips on them and falls, is *Petrocelis franciscana* which forms broad, brownish-red expanses up to 3 feet wide on bare rock surfaces along most any of our rocky headlands. These slippery films crowd off all other vegetation except an endophytic green alga which lives within the tissue. The plant is made up of multitudes of erect filaments in a thick jelly (fig. 30). These can be seen by crushing

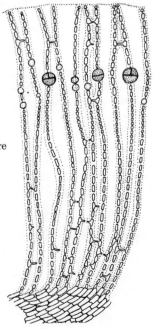

Fig. 30. *Petrocelis* species, microscopic detail of structure and sporangia, × 120.

out a tiny bit on a slide and observing it microscopically, but a scraping of *Petrocelis* is distinguished from brown *Ralfsia* and red *Hildenbrandia* by its gelatinous consistency.

Corallina (small coral)

This is our most widespread jointed calcareous alga and in some areas the most prevalent. The genus is readily recognized by its pinnate branching (see p. 4) which is usually more or less distichous, and by its reproductive conceptacles which are terminal on the segments. The plant is provided flexibility against wave shock by the minute uncalcified pads between the stony segments.

Our largest and most common *Corallina* is *C. officinalis* var. *chilensis,* a variant of the European medicinal corallina of the ancients. It was named *officinalis* by Linnaeus in reference to its favored use as a vermifuge during many centuries prior to 1775.

Bossiella (after Dutch phycologist Madam Weber van Bosse)

Our common species of *Bossiella* are distinguished from *Corallina* by their calcified segments, which have a peculiar wing-nut shape, and by the conceptacles being borne on the faces of these flat segments. *B. dichotoma* (fig. 31) is our most prevalent intertidal species, but there are several others, some of which are dichotomously branched and some pinnately branched. The fresh, living plants are pink, but one often finds in old drift on the beach these jointed corallines made chalky white by sun bleaching.

Calliarthron (beautifully jointed)

Calliarthron cheilosporioides is our largest jointed coralline and may reach a foot in height. The branching is rather loose and sparse, pinnate and opposite to subalternate. *Calliarthron* is somewhat like a large, coarse, pinnate *Bossiella,* but the conceptacles tend to

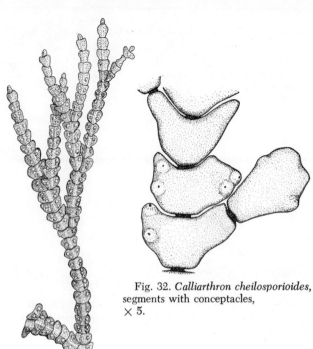

Fig. 32. *Calliarthron cheilosporioides,*
segments with conceptacles,
× 5.

Fig. 31. *Bossiella dichotoma,* upper
portion, × 1.5.

be arranged mainly on the margins of the winged
segments rather than confined to the flat faces (fig.
32). This plant, as well as the bossiellas, is characteristically an inhabitant of lowermost intertidal levels
and will usually be collected only on a good "minus"
tide.

Lithothrix (stone hair)

This genus contains the single species *Lithothrix
aspergillum* which is a common tide-pool inhabitant
in our area. It is finely branched, tufted, and resembles
a coarse shock of bristles. The slender branches, less
than a millimeter thick, are composed of a great many

Fig. 33. *Lithothrix aspergillum,*
small portion with a lateral
conceptacle, × 5.

minute, stony segments only about as long as wide,
and these bear lateral conceptacles (fig. 33).

Male, female, and asexual plants of the various
jointed corallines are so similar that one must usually
look at the contents of the conceptacles for tetraspores, carpospores, or spermatia in order to distinguish the three different plants of the life history.

Melobesia (one of the mythical sea nymphs)

Melobesia mediocris is our smallest calcareous, crustose coralline alga, but one which can be identified
with ease simply because it is an obligate epiphyte on
surf grass. It forms tiny whitish crusts only as wide
as the *Phyllospadix* leaf (fig. 34) and causes such
infected leaves to sparkle with these glistening light
spots in sunlit water. Another common species, *M.
marginata,* lives on various red algae *(Laurencia, Rhodymenia, Gelidium).* Most of the species and genera
of these smaller crustose corallines must be studied
carefully to distinguish them. A hand lens will reveal
the small, mound-like reproductive conceptacles on
the surface of the rounded crusts.

Fig. 34. *Melobesia mediocris*, epiphytic on *Phyllospadix*, × 1.5.

Lithophyllum (stone leaf); *Lithothamnium* (stone branch) The Nullipores

The most widespread of all the marine algae are the rock-inhabiting, crustose corallines of the genera *Lithophyllum* and *Lithothamnium*. Plants of one or the other of these genera occur from the high Arctic and Antarctic through the tropics, from Greenland fjords to Caribbean reefs, from intertidal pools to the uttermost limits of light at depths of up to 500 feet. They may grow as thin, calcareous films only a few cells thick, or as thick, knobby, stony masses widely spreading on rocks and several inches thick. Two representative forms of northern California are shown in figures 35 and 36.

The genera and species of crustose corallines can satisfactorily be identified only by close microscopic examination, and there are few specialists in the world who profess to know this difficult group.

Fig. 35. *Lithothamnium lamellatum,* × 1.

Fig. 36. *Lithophyllum imitans,* × 1.

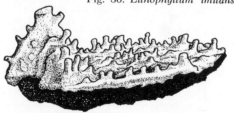

Closely related to *Lithophyllum* and *Lithothamnium* is the strictly tropical genus *Porolithon* to which great importance is attached because of its major role in the amazing biological and geological phenomenon of the coral reef. Coral reefs might better be known as algal reefs, for a majority of them are composed predominantly of calcareous algae. *Porolithon*, in fact, is the principal cementing and binding agent in such reefs and provides for the growth and control of the reef margin. Drill holes thousands of feet deep show that fossil calcareous algal material continues all the way to bedrock.

Polyporolithon (stony bracket fungus—*Polyporous*)

This curious crustose coralline is a readily recognized one, for it grows epiphytically on various jointed corallines as circular or semi-circular plates up to ½ inch in diameter attached by the middle of the lower face (fig. 37). *P. conchatum* and *P. parcum* are two

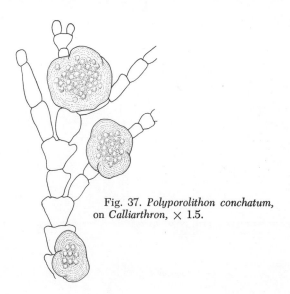

Fig. 37. *Polyporolithon conchatum,* on *Calliarthron*, × 1.5.

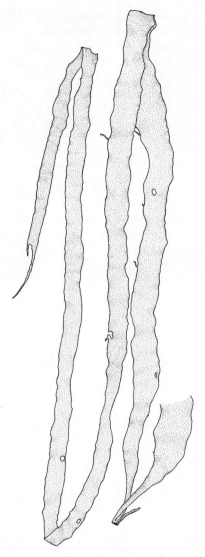

Fig. 38. *Grateloupia doryphora,* × 0.4.

similar species, both very abundant, especially on *Calliarthron*. The thallus of the latter has a very short stalk. *P. conchatum* is sessile.

Grateloupia (after French naturalist Grateloup)

The soft, gelatinous texture and wine-red to purplish color of the long, strap-shaped blades of *Grateloupia doryphora* make it easily recognized (fig. 38). It usually drapes the tops of rocks near and below mean low-water mark. Several blades ordinarily arise from a small, common holdfast and may reach a length of over 4 feet. The margins are sometimes beset with proliferous bladelets. This species occurs both in North and South America and has been named several times from different areas. Our plant is known in some works as *G. californica*.

Prionitis (glistening)

This genus includes several species that characteristically occur in surfy places at low tide levels and below, or in deep tide pools. They are coarse plants

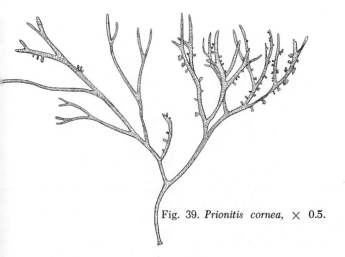

Fig. 39. *Prionitis cornea*, × 0.5.

of narrow, compressed branches, often 2 feet long, of deep, dull purplish-red color and almost cartilaginous texture. The commonest one, *P. lanceolata*, is pinnately branched, but *P. cornea* is primarily dichotomous (fig. 39). A characteristic feature of most species is the presence of irregular series of very short, determinate, pinnate branchlets along the axes and main branches. The internal structure is of densely packed filamentous cells. The cystocarps are deeply embedded and do not project on the surface.

Callophyllis (beautiful leaf)

Befitting its name, these plants are among the most brilliantly colored and attractively branched of our seaweeds. They are usually found in deep waters or at lowermost tide levels where the red phycoerythrin pigment is prominently developed. They are abundant plants of driftweed, and the best specimens may be gathered after a storm. They are mostly flat, thin-bladed species of roughly fan-shaped outline, although some of them are finely dissected. *C. flabellulata* is a

Fig. 40. *Callophyllis flabellulata*, habit, × 1.

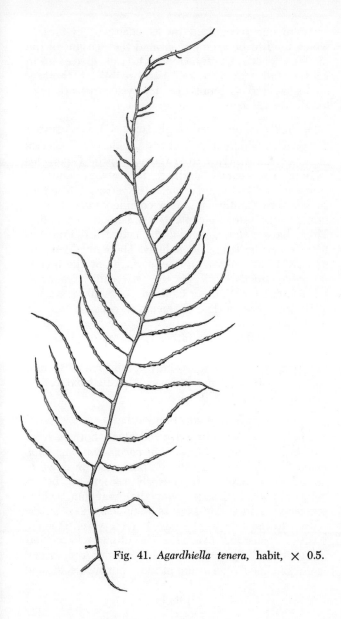

Fig. 41. *Agardhiella tenera*, habit, × 0.5.

common one recognized by its emergent cystocarps which tend to be arranged around the margins of the blades (fig. 40). *C. obtusifolia* is a large species up to 1.5 feet tall with deep red, palmate blades, the segments tapered to blunt tips. Its cystocarps are scattered over the entire blade.

Agardhiella (after Swedish phycologist J. G. Agardh)

Agardhiella tenera (fig. 41) is a widespread species along Pacific America from Canada to the Galapagos Islands. The coarser, northern forms were until recently considered to be a separate species, *A. coulteri*. In northern California it is a common inhabitant of tide pools. Cystocarpic plants are easiest to identify. These have slender, long, fleshy cylindrical branches with few or no lateral branchlets. The embedded cystocarps form bulges on the surface. Sterile plants resemble *Gracilariopsis*, but they are readily separated when a cross section is examined, for *Agardhiella* has a central core of fine filamentous cells within the medulla.

J. G. Agardh and his father C. A. Agardh were the leading European phycologists in Sweden throughout the nineteenth century. Many California seaweeds were described by the younger Agardh from collections made about 1880.

Plocamium (braided hair)

One of our most attractive red algae, both in color and in lacy form, is *Plocamium coccineum* var. *pacificum* (pl. 5), abundant in tide pools and on down to considerable depths. It is easily recognized by its color and its distichous, sympodial branching which is a succession of zig-zags as each main axis is displaced to the side by the next branch which momentarily becomes the main axis. The ultimate branchlets are unilateral. In addition to the common red species is the smaller *P. violaceum* of more purplish color and

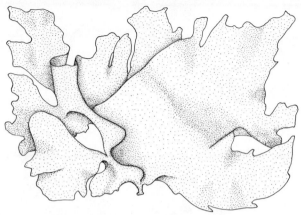

Fig. 42. *Schizymenia pacifica,* habit, × 0.3.

with incurved rather than somewhat recurved branch-lets.

Plocamium makes very fine dry preparations when pressed on white paper. It has long been used as a colorful decoration for greeting cards.

Schizymenia (split membrane)

Schizymenia pacifica is a very slimy-textured, brownish-red alga of lowermost intertidal surfy rocks. The thick, membranous blades are usually broad and 1 to 2 feet long, but much split or lacerated (fig. 42). They arise from an exceedingly short stipe and small holdfast. They are smooth, without any ribs or veins and more or less undulate. One can learn to recognize *Schizymenia* by touch.

Opuntiella (diminutive of *Opuntia*)

Opuntiella californica (fig. 43) is a curiously shaped, rather coarse, cartilaginous alga of deep, dark red color. The broadly-rounded, stiff blades, which arise from the margin of similar parent blades, give the suggestion of the branches of a prickly pear cactus (*Opuntia*). The shape, color, and texture (in com-

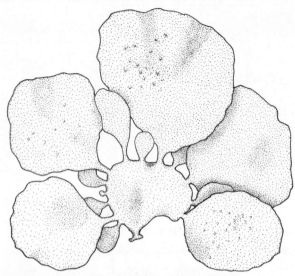

Fig. 43. *Opuntiella californica,* habit, × 0.3.

bination) make this a markedly distinct plant. It will be encountered occasionally in lowermost intertidal areas, but more often in drift.

Gracilariopsis (related to *Gracilaria*)

This interesting, slender, stringy plant is adapted to partial sand burial and grows on stones deeply embedded in sand at low tide levels. The strongly emergent, hemispherical cystocarps distinguish it from *Agardhiella.* Our commonest species is *G. sjoestedtii* (fig. 44) which reaches a length of 6 feet although the cylindrical axes are only about 1/16 of an inch in diameter.

Gracilariopsis is closely related to *Gracilaria,* and both are agarphytes second only to *Gelidium* in commercial importance. Various species are used in different parts of the world. *Gracilaria verrucosa* is an important one which also occurs in California, but is distinguished from *Gracilariopsis sjoestedtii* only by microscopic reproductive characters.

a. An intertidal habitat of green algae (*Ulva*) and brown algae (*Colpomenia*).

b. A tide pool habitat with various red, brown, and green algae.

c. A brown algal habitat (*Egregia* and *Laminaria*) at Avila.

Plate 1

a. A sea grass habitat (*Phyllospadix*) with *Laminaria andersonii* at Avila.

b. Upper intertidal habitat of *Pelvetia* and *Pelvetiopsis* at Pacific Grove.

Plate 2

c. A purplish-colored red alga, *Rhodoglossum affine*.

Plate 3

a. *Polyneura latissima.*

b. *Nienburgia andersoniana.*

Plate 4

a. *Scytosiphon lomentaria.*

b. *Gigartina harveyana.*

Plate 5

a. *Plocamium coccineum* var. *pacificum.*

b. *Gymnogongrus platyphyllus.*

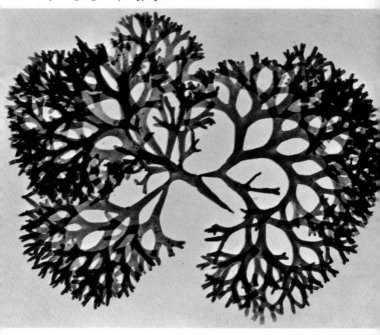

a. *Rhodymenia pacifica.*

Plate 6

b. *Cryptopleura crispa.*

a. *Porphyra perforata.*

b. *Laminaria farlowii.*

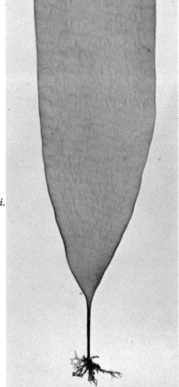

Plate 7

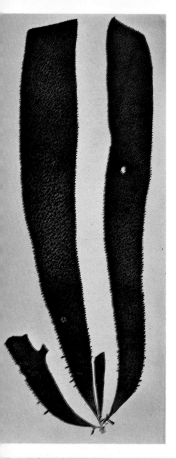

Plate 8

a. *Gigartina spinosa.*

b. *Fauchea laciniata.*

Gymnogongrus (naked swelling)

This is a small genus of flattened plants of regular dichotomous branching and of dense, but parenchymatous structure. Northern California has two rather large species. *G. platyphyllus* (pl. 5) is a rather thin-bladed one compared with *G. linearis* whose segments are quite fleshy and up to 1/16 inch thick. The latter is sometimes very abundant on rocks adjoining sandy beaches where it grows partially buried on rocks embedded in the sand.

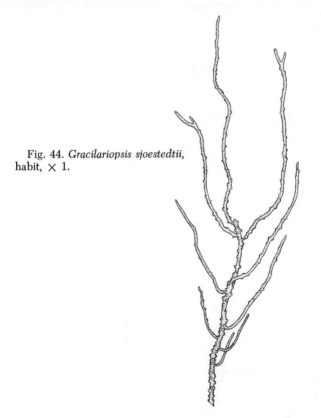

Fig. 44. *Gracilariopsis sjoestedtii,* habit, × 1.

Gigartina (grapestone)

The several common members of this genus are often the most prevalent and conspicuous algae in the lower intertidal zone. Two of the most abundant species, *G. canaliculata* (fig. 45) and *G. papillata*, don't look at all like red algae insofar as color is concerned, for both are very dark purplish to almost black, due to exceedingly dense pigments. Reddish coloration can be detected in younger parts, in thin sections, or by examining the spores. *G. canaliculata* is especially important as one of the commonest rock-cover algae in exposed middle and lower intertidal surfy areas. It is an abundantly and narrowly branched plant 4–8 inches tall with dense, spinulose, determinate branchlets in upper parts. Its morphology is

Fig. 45. *Gigartina canaliculata*, habit, × 1.

the most divergent of any member of the genus in our area. *G. papillata* is a dark, clustered, papillate plant of the higher intertidal, in and around the *Pelvetia* zone.

Most gigartinas are quite distinctly and broadly flattened and are easily recognized by the multitude of minute papillae covering the surfaces of the blades. In the large, blade-like species, such as *G. corymbifera* (fig. 36), *G. harveyana* (pl. 4), and *G. spinosa* (pl. 8), these are especially conspicuous and render the plants easily identified.

Gigartina is an important genus of temperate waters in various parts of the world, and some species reach the largest sizes for red algae. Ours attain 3 feet.

Rhodoglossum (red tongue)

Our only common species of this genus, *Rhodoglossum affine*, is, despite the Latin name, hardly to be compared with a red tongue. It is a dull, reddish-brown or purplish, flat, dichotomously branched plant 3–5 inches tall (pl. 2). It occupies the same exposed rock habitat as *Gigartina canaliculata* and mingles with it. *Rhodoglossum* is closely related to *Gigartina*, but has smooth blades without any superficial papillae.

Also closely related to *R. affine* is the Atlantic *Chondrus crispus*, world famous as Irish Moss and the basis of a great seaweed industry. Irish Moss was originally a product of Europe used in making a kind of milk pudding, but in recent decades has yielded the valuable vegetable-gelatin extract, carrageenin. For this phycocolloid, large quantities of *Chondrus* are harvested in New England and the maritime provinces of Canada. It is widely used as industrial stabilizers and emulsifiers.

Iridaea (iridescent)

Along much of the rocky shore of northern California a major part of the bulk of red algae is made up

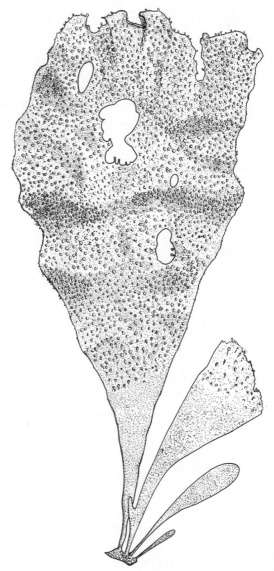

Fig. 46. *Gigartina corymbifera*, habit, × 0.4.

of *Iridaea*, for the plants are both large and abundant. They usually consist of several large, smooth, lanceolate blades 1–2 feet long (fig. 47), but in some cases

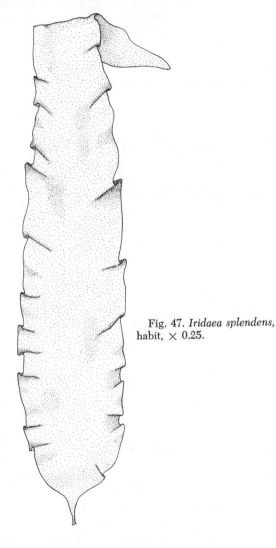

Fig. 47. *Iridaea splendens*, habit, × 0.25.

they reach 4 feet in length. They vary in color from greenish-olive to deep rich purple, and characteristically show a marked iridescence when submerged. Because of variability in form and color, the species are not always easily identified. However, two common ones are *I. flaccidum*, which is our common greenish-colored species, and *I. splendens*, which is the large purple one.

Botryocladia (bladder branch) Sea Grapes

After a winter storm one often finds on the beaches a peculiar seaweed resembling a bunch of red grapes. This is *Botryocladia pseudodichotoma* (fig. 48), which is to be confused with none other of our algae. It grows in the sublittoral, often attached to the holdfasts of *Macrocystis*. The bladders are not filled with air, but with a clear mucilage.

Halosaccion (salt sack) Sea Sacks; Sea Nipples

One of the most curious of our intertidal red algae is *Halosaccion glandiforme* (fig. 49) which grows as a group of erect, slender, water-filled sacks about 1¼ inches in diameter and up to 10 inches long. The plants are usually yellowish or olive-brown, sometimes

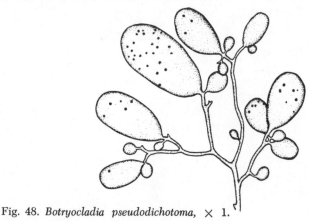

Fig. 48. *Botryocladia pseudodichotoma*, × 1.

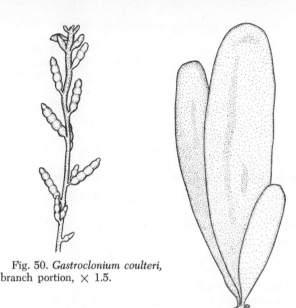

Fig. 50. *Gastroclonium coulteri,*
branch portion, × 1.5.

Fig. 49. *Halosaccion glandiforme,* habit, × 0.5.

reddish purple. When squeezed, these water-filled
sacks will emit several fine jets of water through apical
pores, much to the amusement of those who acci-
dentally discover this property.

Gastroclonium (hollow branch)

This is a genus identified with ease because of its
peculiar ultimate branchlets which are hollow and
provided with diaphragms to form a series of small
chambers (fig. 50). The main axes and branches are
cylindrical and solid. Plants up to 10 inches tall will
be found commonly on rocks throughout much of the
middle and lower intertidal zones. A closely related
genus, *Coeloseira,* also with these chambered branchlets, looks like a diminutive edition of *Gastroclonium*
only 1 inch high or less.

[71]

Rhodymenia (red membrane)

Color in *Rhodymenia* is true to its name. Always pink or red, these small, dichotomously branched, digitate or fan-shaped blades are commonly found at lowest tide levels on vertical rock faces on in clefts and crevices where the light is subdued and there is limited exposure to air. There are two common species. *R. californica* looks like a small edition of the larger *R. pacifica* (pl. 6) which reaches 3 to 5 inches. Both species range down into the sublittoral to depths of 20–25 feet.

Rhodymenia has a strictly parenchymatous structure. Another distinctive feature of our two common species is the presence of spreading stolons from the base of the stipe.

Fauchea (after French naturalist Fauche)

Fauchea laciniata (pl. 8) is an example of one of the brightly colored red algae which are so sensitive to air exposure that they seldom are found in intertidal situations. On the other hand, they are sometimes abundant in deeper waters, and after a storm may be strewn along a beach, neatly spread out on the sand. Compared with *Rhodymenia, Fauchea* is soft and lubricous. The cystocarps bear a distinctive crown of pointed lobes.

Centroceras (horns around a center)

There is one widespread species of this genus, *C. clavulatum*, originally described from Peru, but now known throughout the temperate and tropical Pacific. We encounter it commonly on intertidal rocks as dull reddish tufts and mats 1–3 inches tall. It is somewhat harsh to the touch. The cylindrical axes are regularly dichotomous and strongly incurved at the tips. They are minutely segmented and each segment bears projecting spines which are clearly visible with a lens

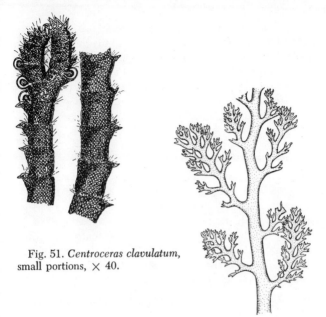

Fig. 51. *Centroceras clavulatum,* small portions, × 40.

Fig. 52. *Microcladia coulteri,* midportion of an axis, × 4.

(fig. 51). These provide the rough texture. The plant tends to fragment at the joints when it dies or is preserved.

Microcladia (small branches)

This is one of our commonest and most attractive epiphytes. It is a finely branched, delicate plant of rose-red color that may reach a foot in length, but is attached to *Gigartina, Prionitis,* or other coarse red algae. *M. coulteri* (fig. 52) is the commonest species. The branching is regularly alternate and distichous. The whole plant has a somewhat pyramidal shape. It reaches its best development on host plants in subtidal waters, and the finest specimens will be encountered in drift.

[73]

Ptilota (Greek, pinnated)

Ptilota is another of our attractive, bright red, finely, distichously branched plants suggesting the frond of a fern. *P. filicina* (fig. 53) is one of our common species which may be found on rocks at low tide levels, but is often abundant in drift weed. The plants are

Fig. 53. *Ptilota filicina*, detail of lateral branch, × 4.

usually 6 to 12 inches tall and are best recognized by using a hand lens to note that the ultimate branchlets are opposite, but that one member of each pair is quite large and the other very small. The larger ultimate branch has tiny marginal teeth.

Nienburgia (after German phycologist Nienburg)

Nienburgia andersoniana (pl. 3) is one of our interesting representatives of the algal family Delesseriaceae which contains some of the most colorful and attractive of the membranous algae. This one consists of narrow, branched blades with a midrib in lower parts and with conspicuously toothed margins. It varies considerably in width and stature but reaches a foot in length. It grows on lower littoral rocks, often in company with *Rhodymenia* and sometimes protected by hanks of sea-grass leaves.

A majority of the Delesseriaceae are plants of lowermost tide levels or deeper waters, and some extend to depths of 200–300 feet. Many are characterized by intricate vein patterns suggesting those of higher plants.

Polyneura (many veins)

This is a brightly colored red alga of lowermost intertidal rocks in somewhat sheltered situations. It is often conspicuous in drift. The anastomosing veins of the membranous blades are unique and make it easy to identify. The only species is *P. latissima* (pl. 3) which ranges from Canada to Mexico. The plants are delicate and often are found in tattered, lacerated condition, but occasionally perfect examples up to a foot tall may be collected, and these make admirable mounted specimens. The reproductive bodies are scattered over the surfaces of the blades.

Cryptopleura (hidden ribs)

Several common species of this genus occur intertidally or in drift along northern California. They are membranous forms with ligulate, subdichotomous blades bearing a heavy midrib below and microscopic

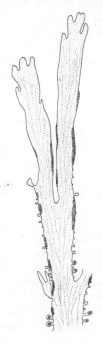

Fig. 54. *Cryptopleura violacea,* upper part showing marginal bladelets, veins, and sporangial sori, × 0.9.

veins above. The blade margins are characteristically provided with ruffles and (or) small fertile bladelets. *C. violacea* is a large, saxicolous species 5–10 inches tall, of purplish color, with rather few marginal outgrowths, but with elongate tetrasporangial sori borne within the blade margins (fig. 54). *C. crispa* (pl. 6) is an occasional epiphytic species. *C. ruprechtianum* is a large plant up to a foot long with abundant marginal leaflets. A similar, but still larger plant, is *Botryoglossum farlowianum* in which the marginal leaflets are exceedingly abundant, small, and congested.

Hymenena (like a membrane)

These are thin, membranous plants 8–12 inches tall of very low tide levels. They consist of palmate or fan-shaped blades divided into many segments. The veins diverge outwardly, and the tetrasporangial sori form slender patches in line with the veins. *H. flabelligera* (fig. 55) is our commonest species. Hymenenas differ also from cryptopleuras in lacking the abundant small marginal leaflets along the blades.

Polysiphonia (many tubes)

Polysiphonia is one of the familiar names among marine algae, for these plants have long been used in biology classes as examples of the Rhodophyta. This has been so not only because they are common and widely available for instructive microscopic examination, but because *Polysiphonia* was the first red alga in which the life history was conclusively worked out half a century ago. The name refers to the multiple, often elongate and tube-like cells (pericentral cells) arranged in a cylinder around a central axial cell and, all being the same length, forming a series of "polysiphonous" segments.

A number of species of *Polysiphonia* occur in northern California of which some are common. They are usually small, short, tufted forms or delicate epiphytes,

[76]

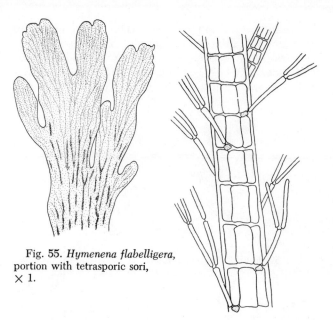

Fig. 55. *Hymenena flabelligera*,
portion with tetrasporic sori,
× 1.

Fig. 56. *Polysiphonia* species, showing arrangement of pericentral cells in midportion of an axis, and colorless hairs,
× 200.

but *P. paniculata* and *P. pacifica* reach 6 to 8 inches
in length. The ends of the branches are almost always
provided with fine, colorless hairs. A hand lens may
reveal these and the tiers of pericentral cells (fig. 56),
but a compound microscope is needed to make specific
identifications.

Pterosiphonia (wing tube)

This is another delicate form closely related to *Polysiphonia* but more readily identified. The commonest
species, *P. dendroidea*, is a tufted intertidal, rock-
inhabiting form. It is deep, dull red to almost blackish,
1–3 inches long, and consists of distichous, pinnate

branchlets on a flattened axis. The individual main axes look like minute feathers (fig. 57). The structure of pericentral cells is comparable with *Polysiphonia*. *P. baileyi* is a larger, black, coarse form to 6 inches tall or more with less delicate pinnae.

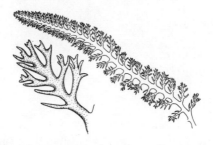

Fig. 57. *Pterosiphonia dendroidea,* showing one of the feather-like branches, × 3.5, and a lateral branchlet in detail, × 35.

Pterochondria (wing *Chondria,* a related alga)

Pterochondria woodii (fig. 58) is another common epiphyte of *Cystoseira* on which it is often abundant during spring to early autumn. It may also live on various other coarse algae. It is a finely-branched, distichous plant with regularly alternate branches, but without percurrent axes. Except for the latter feature and its epiphytic habit, it somewhat suggests *Pterosiphonia*.

Laurencia (after French naturalist de la Laurencie)

Most algae are recognized by their structural and morphological characters. A few have distinctive textures. This one is identifiable by smell. Unfortunately, the peculiar acrid odor is difficult to describe, and it must be learned before the plants can be recognized in the dark.

Laurencia is a genus of variable morphology. We have common examples both of cylindrical and flat-

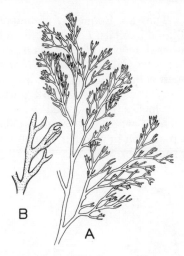

Fig. 58. *Pterochondria woodii*, habit, × 3.5, and detail of an ultimate branch, × 16.

Fig. 59. *Laurencia spectabilis*, habit, × 1.

tened forms. They are frequently abundant in middle and lower littoral habitats. *L. spectabilis*, a quite large, pinnate, flattened species (fig. 59) is especially widespread in northern California. *L. pacifica* is probably our commonest cylindrical species, at least as far north as Santa Cruz. It is a bushy, dark purplish, fleshy plant several inches tall covered with very short, stubby branchlets which give it a papillate appearance. The tip of each branch has a minute indentation or pit. This sunken growing point (fig. 60) often bears a tuft of microscopic hairs.

Fig. 60 *Laurencia* species, showing apical pit, × 23.

Odonthalia (tooth branch)

This is a genus characteristic of Canadian and Alaska shores. *O. floccosa* is a southern species well represented in northern California. It reaches 1½ feet in height and is of a blackish-brown color. The major branches are slender and subcylindrical. They bear alternate, distichous short branchlets which in turn bear short, flat, and pointed ultimate branchlets. These latter are usually clustered in groups (fig. 61).

[80]

Fig. 61. *Odonthalia floccosa*, lateral branch with branchlets, × 1.

Rhodomela (red to black)

This is another red alga which ranges from our territory all the way to the Bering Sea. It is brownish black to black. The common species *R. larix* (fig. 62) consists of several wiry axes to about 8 inches long closely beset with spirally arranged clusters of cylindrical branchlets about ¼ inch long. These plants are characteristic inhabitants of middle intertidal rocks and sometimes form a dominant part of the vegetation.

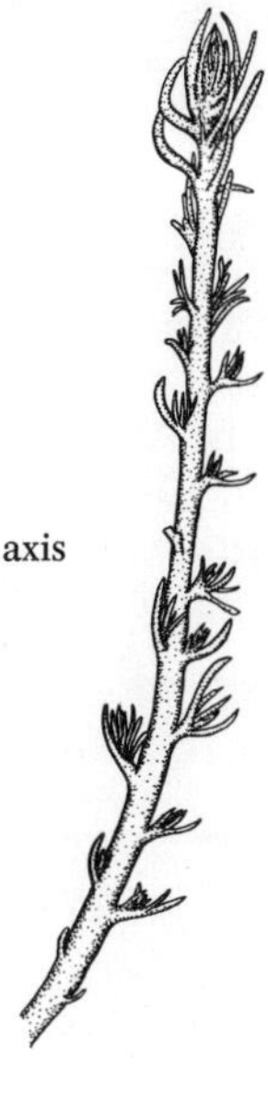

Fig. 62. *Rhodomela larix*, a young axis in which the ultimate branchlets are much less congested than in older plants, × 1.5.

Dawson, E. Y., 1956. How to Know the Seaweeds. 197 pp., 259
figs. Wm. C. Brown Co., Dubuque, Iowa.

————, 1965. Some marine algae in the vicinity of Humboldt
State College, Humboldt County, California. 78 pp.,
Humboldt State College.

Setchell, W. A., and N. L. Gardner, 1920-1925. The marine al-
gae of the Pacific Coast of North America. Pt. 2,
Chlorophyceae; Pt. 3, Melanophyceae. Univ. of Calif.
Publ. Bot. 8: 139-898, 95 pls.

Smith, G. M. 1944. Marine algae of the Monterey Peninsula,
California. ix + 622 pp., 98 pls. Stanford Univ. Press.
(This includes about two-thirds of all the species
known from northern California.)

THE SEA GRASSES

Although the vast majority of seashore plants are
algae, there are many coastal localities at which one
will find at least one kind of flowering plant growing
under strictly marine conditions in intertidal waters
or below. Sometimes these sea grasses may be so abundant as to form extensive beds on sand, mud or rocks
to the virtual exclusion of other kinds of plants.

Inasmuch as only three kinds of sea grasses occur
in northern California, a key to them is unnecessary
and they may be identified by the illustrations and
notes that follow.

Zostera (a girdle or band) Eel Grass

The true Eel Grass, *Zostera marina,* is a plant of
quiet waters. It commonly lives on tidal mud flats and
in bays and estuaries from low tide level down to
twenty feet or more. The illustrations in figure 62
show three variants of eel grass of which those on the
left represent narrow-leaved forms characteristic of

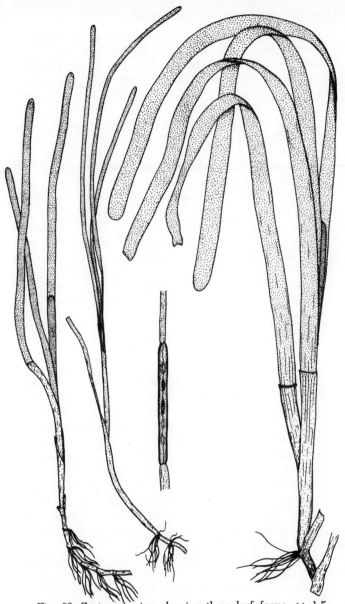

Fig. 63. *Zostera marina*, showing three leaf forms, × 1.5, part of a fertile stem, × 1.

sheltered bays and salt marshes, such as Elkhorn Slough, San Francisco Bay, and Tomales Bay. The large, broad-leaf form shown is known as var. *latifolia* and occurs on sheltered sandy bottoms along the open coast. Fragments of these plants are commonly cast up on sandy beaches.

The flowers and fruits of eel grass are rather obscure. Part of a fertile stem is shown in figure 63, and two developing seeds are visible where the enveloping spathe does not completely cover them.

Because eel grass is an important food plant of certain birds and of many marine animals, it received a great deal of attention some years ago following its almost complete disappearance from the Atlantic Coast in 1931-1932. The significance of this destructive "wasting disease" of *Zostera* led to much research toward determining its cause, but this never was convincingly accomplished. It took fifteen years for the eel grass to return to normal growth, and there has not since been any so serious a decline.

Phyllospadix (leaf inflorescence) Surf Grass

Two species of Surf Grass occur widely along the Pacific Coast. Unlike *Zostera*, these plants normally grow in rocky places on surfy shores, from intertidal levels down to as much as 50 feet. *P. torreyi* (fig. 64) has narrow, compressed, somewhat wiry leaves and long flowering stems bearing several spadices as shown in the figure. *P. scouleri* has thinner, shorter leaves and short, basal flowering stems bearing only one or two spadices. It is especially abundant in intertidal situations and forms extensive emerald green masses on rocky shores near mean low tide line (pl. 2). Both of these plants are commonly mistaken by the layman for eel grass.

The seaweed collector should not overlook the importance of surf grass as a habitat for various kinds of algae. Not only do epiphytic species occur regularly on it (*Melobesia; Smithora*) but others are hidden

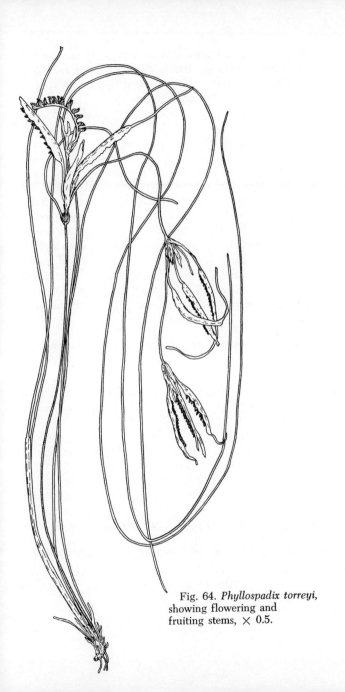

Fig. 64. *Phyllospadix torreyi*, showing flowering and fruiting stems, × 0.5.

beneath the protecting layer of leaves. If one simply spreads and opens up the mantle of leaves to reveal the inhabitants under them, he will find many species otherwise passed over unseen.

COASTAL SALT-MARSH VEGETATION

Apart from the strictly marine plants, which are those regularly and completely submerged by the sea water, are those seashore plants referred to as halophytes, or salt plants, which live in marine marshes where they are only partially or occasionally inundated by the sea. These are flowering plants adapted to growth in salty soil. We have a number of interesting forms along northern California in the marshes around Morro Bay, Moss Landing, San Francisco Bay, Tomales Bay, Humboldt Bay, etc. A few will be mentioned below.

Salicornia (salt horn) Pickle Weed; Glasswort

The most conspicuous of our common halophytes is *Salicornia* which is impressionable because of its peculiar succulent, jointed stems. Both annual and perennial species occur, but they are similar in appearance and rather difficult to identify specifically because of their exceedingly obscure flowers. *S. virginica* is our abundant perennial species (fig. 65). *S. europea* is the commonest annual one.

Salicornia has had a long tradition of utilization in Europe as a fresh vegetable or as a pickle plant. So palatable are some of the species that in certain of the older horticultural works it was recommended that they be cultivated as a vegetable by imitating a portion of a salt marsh. Due to their high yield of soda, several species were formerly used in making glass and soap, the ashes of the Glasswort being known in the trade as barilla.

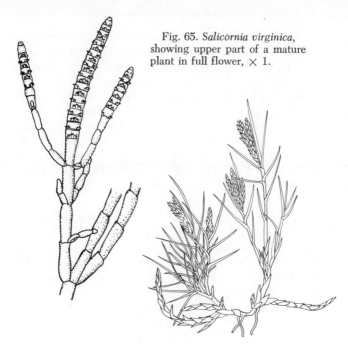

Fig. 65. *Salicornia virginica,* showing upper part of a mature plant in full flower, × 1.

Fig. 66. *Distichlis spicata,* habit, × 0.4.

Distichlis (two-ranked) Salt Grass

The commonest halophytic grass along salt marshes and sandy flats of northern California is *Distichlis spicata* (fig. 66). Salt Grass is a perennial plant consisting of extensive creeping, scaly rhizomes from which stiff, harsh, and somewhat spiny leaves arise to form dense colonies. Barefoot beach-goers remember the plant well after having a stickery experience of walking on it. It tends to grow at the margins of marshes or above normal high tide line on the shore where only unusually high water may cover it. The plants are ordinarily low and spreading, 3 to 4 inches tall, but may sometimes bunch up to a foot high.

Spartina (from Greek, a cord) Cord Grass

The stout, bushy, coarse grass of our salt marshes, with leaves up to half an inch broad at the base, is the California Cord Grass, *Spartina foliosa* (fig. 67). This is a plant one to three feet high, of marsh waterways in which the tide inundates it often to half or more its stature. Thus, at high water *Spartina* stands partially submerged like rice in a paddy. The leafy stems arise from extensive creeping rhizomes buried in the salty mud. The inflorescences are dense, spikelike structures 6 to 8 inches long.

Frankenia (after Swedish botanist Johann Franke, 1590-1661)

The only abundant plant of our salt marshes that bears noticeable flowers is *Frankenia grandiflora* (fig. 68), but even these "grand" pink flowers are only $\frac{5}{8}$ of an inch across. When in full bloom, however, they are attractive and lend a modicum of bright color to the varied shades of green on the marsh. *Frankenia* is a low bush 4 to 16 inches tall with its short, narrow leaves in groups. This plant, like *Distichlis*, also inhabits the salt marsh margins where the soil is infrequently covered with salt water.

Suaeda (the Arabic name) Sea-Blite

Our common marsh *Suaeda* from Morro Bay to San Francisco Bay is *S. californica* (fig. 69) which is a fleshy, dull gray, decumbent to semi-erect bush 3 feet or more wide and up to 1–3 feet tall. The leaves are simple and linear, about half an inch long and usually densely clothed with microscopic, downy hairs. The flowers are small, clustered and obscure, without any colored petals.

Several other species of *Suaeda* occur in California marshes, but most inhabit inland alkaline flats.

Fig. 67. *Spartina foliosa*, part of an axis with leaves, × 0.5.

Fig. 68. *Frankenia grandiflora*, flower, × 4; habit, × 0.4.

Fig. 69. *Suaeda californica*, habit, × 0.5; a flower, × 3.5.

COASTAL STRAND VEGETATION

The student of seashore plants cannot help but notice in his visits to the beaches and reefs for collection of algae, that there are a number of plants peculiar to the slightly elevated terrestrial margins of the sea. This region of the shore, known as the coastal strand, includes environments not generally subject to inundation by seawater (as are the marine areas, proper, and the marshes) but nonetheless influenced by the adjoining sea by manner of salt spray, mist, fog, blowing and drifting sand, etc. A number of the plants there are especially adapted to life in shoreside dunes or in the uppermost reaches of sand beaches. Several of the common and conspicuous plants of the coastal strand are pointed out and depicted below.

Abronia (graceful) Sand Verbena

Perhaps the most colorful of the dune plants are the sand verbenas of which we have three common kinds: the rose-flowered A. *umbellata* (as far north as Sonoma County), the yellow-flowered A. *latifolia* (throughout northern California), and the crimson-flowered A. *maritima* (in San Luis Obispo County) (fig. 70). These are all perennial, prostrate herbs with opposite leaves ānd rather thick, succulent stems. The roots are usually stout and fleshy, deeply embedded in the sand. The most characteristic feature of the herbage is its covering with minute glandular hairs which exude a sticky material to which grains of sand adhere. Thus the plants appear to be sprinkled with sand, but one finds that the sand does not shake off. The flowers are fragrant and are borne in dense clusters. The flowering season is long, extending from February to October or November.

Fig. 70. *Abronia maritima*, habit, × 0.5.; flower and fruit.

Fig. 71. *Oenothera cheiranthifolia*, habit, × 0.5; mature fruit, × 1.

Oenothera (wine scenting) Evening Primrose

The evening primrose of the northern California coastal strand is the yellow-flowered *O. cheiranthifolia*. This is a plant of silvery pubescent foliage which consists of a basal rosette of thick, oblanceolate leaves from which several prostrate or decumbent stems radiate for 4 to 20 inches. The flowers are quite large, with bright yellow petals up to an inch long, sometimes with reddish spots. They appear in spring and continue throughout the summer. The fruiting capsules become peculiarly coiled at maturity (fig. 71).

Atriplex (ancient Latin name) Salt Bush

The salt bushes are characteristic plants of alkaline sinks, dry lakes, and saline areas throughout the West. Several species occur in our coastal salt marshes and we have others along the northern California sea beaches and coastal strand. A common one is *A. leucophylla* (fig. 72). Some of the inland salt bushes and weedy forms that appear in waste places are naturalized from Eurasia and from Australia.

These are mostly dull-looking shrubs of grayish or whitish color. They bear separate male and female flowers which are obscure, small structures without colored parts. There is nothing glamorous or striking about the salt bushes, but they are often a prevalent component of the seashore vegetation and should be recognized for their importance in this narrowly restricted terrestrial environment which adjoins the marine environment.

Mesembryanthemum (midday flower) Ice Plant

This is a very large genus of succulent plants native to southern hemisphere regions, particularly South Africa, where hundreds of species provide some of the most colorful natural ground covers in the world. Because of their abundant flowers, often of striking

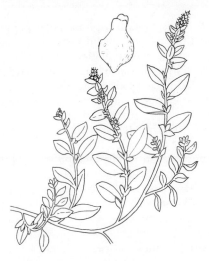

Fig. 72. *Atriplex leucophylla*, habit, × 0.5; fruit, × 3.

Fig. 73. *Mesembryanthemum crystallinum,* × 3.

brilliance, the ice plants have long been popular garden plants in the warm, coastal regions of California. They have also been used widely as sand-stabilizing and erosion-control plants wherever a drought-resistant succulent can be used. From these plantings the ice plants have escaped and become naturalized along the California shore. Several of them are especially well adapted to compete with the vegetation of the coastal strand, so that we find them frequently spreading over upper beach sands, trailing over bluffs, and covering soils just above high tide line.

The true Ice Plant is *Mesembryanthemum crystallinum* (fig. 73) so called because of its very large vesicular cells covering the surface of the stems and leaves and giving it the sparkling appearance of being adorned with globules of ice. It is an annual plant with broad, ovate leaves which are green and very succulent in spring. In summer the older plants become reddish and the leaves reduced. The flowers are white or pinkish and not especially striking.

The more conspicuous succulents that are generally called ice plants, but more correctly Sea Fig or Hottentot Fig, are two species with elongate, succulent leaves of trangular shape in cross section. These are the creeping, deep green, fleshy plants so widely used as roadside binders and as erosion-control plants on dry slopes. We have the red-flowered one (*M. chilense*) native of South America, and a yellow-flowered one (*M. edule*) native of South Africa (fig. 74). The latter was traditionally a food plant of the Hottentots, since the fruits are edible.

Several other species have become naturalized on sea bluffs and low ground along the shore. Although all have succulent leaves, the leaves of different species are unlike in form and appearance. The flowers, however, whether white, rose, purple, or yellow, are all similar in their wheel-like shape, numerous, slender petals, and abundant stamens.

Fig. 74. *Mesembryanthemum edule,* × 0.5.

Haplopappus (simple pappus) Mock Heather

Haplopappus ericoides is one of our small shrubby composites characteristically inhabiting coastal sand dunes. It is a compact, somewhat resinous, heather-like shrub 1–3 feet high with many erect branchlets bearing numerous slender, subterete leaves ½ inch long or less (fig. 75). The small yellow flower heads are produced abundantly during late summer (Aug.–Sept.) and are followed by ripe seed heads with white pappus bristles. These plants may be observed along much of the coast from Marin County south. They are especially prevalent among dunes.

Fig. 75. *Haplopappus ericoides*, habit, × 1.

Fig. 76. *Convolvulus soldanella*, habit, × 0.3.

Convolvulus (to entwine) Beach Morning Glory

The morning glory of our beaches *(Convolvulus soldanella)* is another of our naturalized plants from the Old World. This pinkish or purplish-flowered one blooms from April to August along the coastal strand, living perennially from deep-seated rootstocks and producing fleshy, prostrate stems ½ to 1½ feet long from the root crown (fig. 76). The leaves are thick and somewhat fleshy. Not only do we find it along the California coast, but it extends north to Washington and occurs also in South America and on many other Pacific sea shores.

SOME REFERENCES TO
NORTHERN CALIFORNIA SEASHORE PLANTS
OTHER THAN MARINE ALGAE

Dawson, E. Y., 1956. How to Know the Seaweeds, 197 pp., 259 figs. Wm. C. Brown Co., Dubuque, Iowa.

Mason, H. L., 1957. A Flora of the Marshes of California. 878 pp., 367 figs. Univ. of California Press.

Munz, P. A., 1963. A California Flora. 1681 pp., 134 figs. Univ. of California Press.

GLOSSARY

agarphyte: an alga from which agar can be obtained.

alternation of generation: the reproduction by organisms that do not necessarily or precisely resemble the parent, but the grandparent; applied especially to the regular succession of gametophyte and sporophyte phases.

anastomosing: joined or united like the parts of a network.

apical cell: a single cell; at the apex of a thallus or its branch from which growth emanates.

articulated coralline: a calcareous alga of the family Corallinaceae in which the stony segments are separted by minute uncalcified, flexible joints.

axial filament: a cellular filament or strand running in the morphological axis of a thallus.

blade: the more or less broad, flattened, foliose part of an erect alga.

carpospore: a kind of sport in the red algae developing usually within a cystocarp which arises after sexual fusion on the female gametophyte plant.

coenocyte: a term traditionally applied to an alga with multinucleate cell or cells.

compressed: somewhat flattened so that the cross section is elliptical.

conceptacle: a cavity opening to the thallus surface and containing reproductive organs.

coralline: one of the calcareous algae of the family Corallinaceae.

coronate: with points like a crown.

crustose: in the form of a crust.

cystocarp: the "fruit" resulting from fertilization in Rhodophytha, usually bearing carpospores within a pericarp.

decumbent: lying down, but with the tip ascending.

determinate: having limited growth.

dichotomous: forked.

digitate: resembling the fingers of a hand.

distichous: in two ranks.

emergent: protruding prominently.

entire: without marginal teeth or serrations.

epiphyte: a plant that grows on another plant.

gametophyte: a plant that produces gametes.

habit: the gross aspect of a plant.

haptera: basal outgrowths that form part of a holdfast.

holdfast: the basal attachment organ of an alga.

hydrophilic: having a great affinity for water.

hygroscopic: readily absorbing and retaining moisture.

inflorescence: an aggregation of flowers clustered together in a particular manner.

lanceolate: shaped like a lance head.

linear: long and narrow.

lubricous: slimy or slippery.

medulla: the central or median tissue region of a thallus.

meristem: the point or region from which active growth takes place.

oblanceolate: inversely lance-shaped.

obligate epiphyte: living in such close relationship on another plant that no alternate habitat is acceptable.

palmate: hand-shaped.

papilla: a small superficial protuberance.

papillate: provided with papillae.

pappus: a crown of bristles at the summit of the seed in Compositae.

parenchymatous: resembling parenchyma; consisting of comparatively thin-walled cells of more or less isodiametrical form.

pedicellate: provided with a stalk or pedicel.

percurrent: running through to the end.

pericentral cell: one of a ring of cells cut off from and surrounding a central (axial) cell in the red algae.

phycocolloid: a colloidal substance obtained from seaweeds.

phycologist: one who studies algae.

phylum: one of the largest divisions or categories of the plant or animal kingdoms by which organisms are classified.

pinnae: the individual divisions or parts of a pinnate axis.

pinnate: having the divisions arranged on each side of a common rachis: featherlike.

pneumatocyst: an air-float bladder

polystichous: in several to many ranks.

proliferous: showing the development of regenerative offshoots, ordinarily in the sense of unusual position or abundance.

pubescent: covered with soft, short hairs; downy.

pulvinate: cushion-shaped.

radial: regularly arranged about a central axis.

recurved: curved back or down.

rhizome: a rootstock or dorsiventral stem, usually prostrate, producing roots as well as stems or leaves.

saxicolous: growing on rocks.

secund: arranged along one side of an axis.

segment: one of the divisions of a jointed, segmented, or divided thallus.

septum: a wall or partition.

septate: provided with walls or partitions.

simple: unbranched.

sinuous: of serpentine or wavy form.

sorus (sori): a group or cluster of reproductive organs.

spadix (spadices): a kind of flower spike with a fleshy axis.

spathe: a large bract enclosing a flower cluster (spadix).

spermatium: a non-motile male gamete in the red algae.

spike: an inflorescence with sessile flowers on an axis.

spinulose: provided with diminutive spines.

sporangium: a structure in which spores are produced.

sporophyll: a leaf-like, spore-producing blade.

sporophyte: a plant that produces spores, generally the generation alternating with the gametophyte.

stipe: the stem-like, usually basal part of a thallus.

stipitate: provided with a stipe.

stolon: a horizontal, root-like stem that attaches at the tip.

subdichotomous: somewhat or almost dichotomous.

subterete: somewhat or almost cylindrical.

sympodial: a mode of development in which the apparent main axis is not developed by continuous terminal growth, but is made up of successive secondary axes, each representing a branch.

tetraspore: a spore formed in a group of four in a tetrasporangium.

thallus: the whole plant body of an alga.

undulate: wavy.

uniseriate: consisting of a single row or series.

verticillate: arising in a whorl from a single point of attachment.

zoospore: a motile spore with one or more flagella or cilia by the vibration of which it swims.

INDEX